Grace Kelly

ICON OF STYLE TO ROYAL BRIDE

Grace Kelly

ICON OF STYLE TO ROYAL BRIDE

H. Kristina Haugland

Philadelphia Museum of Art
in association with
Yale University Press
New Haven and London

This book is published on the occasion of the exhibition *Fit for a Princess: Grace Kelly's Wedding Dress* at the Philadelphia Museum of Art from April 1 to May 21, 2006.

The exhibition is supported by a generous gift from Carol Ware Gates in honor of Marian S. Ware. The accompanying publication is also supported by the Laura and William C. Buck Endowment for Special Publications and The Women's Committee of the Philadelphia Museum of Art.

Front cover: © Bettmann/CORBIS (p. 59)
Back cover: © Bettmann/CORBIS (p. 21)
Frontispiece: After the cathedral wedding, Princess Grace and Prince Rainier stride down the Galerie d'Hercule of the palace. Archives Detaille/SIPA

Produced by the Publishing Department
Philadelphia Museum of Art
2525 Pennsylvania Avenue
Philadelphia, PA 19130
USA
www.philamuseum.org

Published by the Philadelphia Museum of Art in association with Yale University Press
P.O. Box 209040
302 Temple Street
New Haven, CT 06520
www.yalebooks.com

Edited by Beth A. Huseman
Production by Richard Bonk
Designed by Andrea Hemmann/GHI Design
Drawings by woolypear
Separations, printing, and binding by
Amilcare Pizzi, S.P.A., Milan

Note to the reader: Citations and sources can be found on pages 77–80.

Library of Congress Cataloging-in-Publication Data

Haugland, Kristina (H. Kristina), 1959-
    Grace Kelly : icon of style to royal bride /
H. Kristina Haugland.
        p. cm.
    Includes bibliographical references.
    ISBN 0-87633-193-2 (paper)
    ISBN 0-300-11644-6 (Yale : paper)
    1. Wedding costume—California—Hollywood (Los Angeles) 2. Grace, Princess of Monaco, 1929-1982—Clothing. 3. Rose, Helen, 1904-1985. 4. Metro-Goldwyn-Mayer. I. Title.
GT1753.U6H38 2006
392.5'4—dc22

                                    2005037164

FOREWORD

I t is a pleasure for the Philadelphia Museum of Art to publish this celebration of one of the most famous and popular treasures in its collection of almost 30,000 examples of costume, fashion, and textile art, upon the occasion of the fiftieth anniversary of the wedding of Grace Kelly of Philadelphia to Prince Rainier III of Monaco on April 19, 1956. Her classic and elegant wedding dress was the bride's thoughtful gift to the Museum and has become an icon of restrained Hollywood elegance just as she is an icon of American film. H. Kristina Haugland, Associate Curator of Costume and Textiles, has told the story of the dress and its beautiful owner with vivid detail and panache, and we join her in expressing heartfelt thanks to members of the extended Kelly family and their friends for their generosity, especially Meg Davis Packer, Grace Kelly's niece, whose flower girl ensemble is owned by the Museum, and Mrs. Joseph S. Rambo, who donated her bridesmaid dress as well as the dress she wore to a pre-wedding gala. Marilyn Evins and Reed Evins, respectively the widow and nephew of shoe designer David Evins, and Jeanie Beenk, sister of Joseph Hong, who designed the attendants' dresses, also deserve our warm gratitude for providing information for the catalogue.

Beth A. Huseman of the Museum's Publishing Department worked with boundless energy and creativity as the editor of this book, which was given its appropriately elegant design by Andrea Hemmann. The Museum is particularly pleased that this title marks the beginning of a newly forged relationship with our co-publisher, Yale University Press.

We owe a debt of gratitude to Carol Ware Gates, who helped make the exhibition possible through a generous gift in honor of her mother, Marian S. Ware. This catalogue is the first to be supported by a newly created endowment for publications established by Laura and William C. Buck. Our sincere appreciation goes to the Bucks for their contribution toward this book and future publications. Without the generous and farsighted support of the Women's Committee of the Museum, all too few exciting projects—including this book—could ever be realized. We extend most enthusiastic thanks to Trustee Barbara B. Aronson, who chairs the Costume and Textiles Committee, and her husband, Theodore, for their wide-ranging support of costume and textiles and so many other Museum initiatives.

As this book appears in the spring of 2006, it also marks an exciting time at the Museum when the venerable yet lively Department of Costume and Textiles, among the oldest and largest in an American museum, prepares to move into handsome and spacious new quarters in the Museum's Ruth and Raymond G. Perelman Building across Kelly Drive (named for Grace Kelly's beloved brother, the talented athlete and city councilman John B. Kelly, Jr.) from the Museum's neo-classical building on Fairmount. The new Hamilton Center for Costume and Textiles, the Joan and Bernard Spain Gallery, and a capacious conservation laboratory, all now under construction in the Perelman Building, await this distinguished collection and the public it will serve, educate, and delight.

Anne d'Harnoncourt
The George D. Widener Director
and Chief Executive Officer

Dilys E. Blum
Curator of Costume and Textiles

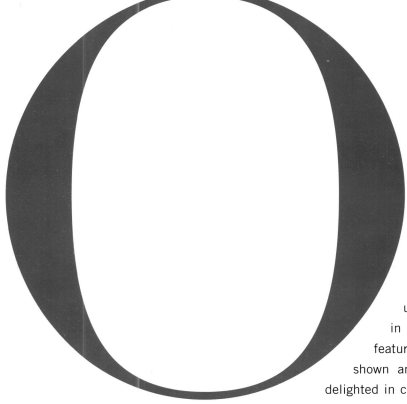

ON APRIL 19, 1956, MILLIONS OF PEOPLE around the world participated vicariously in the wedding of twenty-six-year-old Philadelphia-born film star Grace Kelly and Prince Rainier III of Monaco. In the Monégasque cathedral that morning, the beautiful, radiant bride wore a "fairy-tale" wedding gown that had been the subject of intense interest since the announcement of the couple's engagement more than three months before. Designed by Helen Rose and made under top-secret conditions by Metro-Goldwyn-Mayer in Hollywood, the lace and silk bridal gown was featured on the front pages of newspapers nationwide and shown and discussed in every form of media, which had delighted in covering each detail of the royal wedding. Before her engagement, Grace Kelly had already been big news for several years, rising meteorically in her film career to become a top box-office draw and an Academy Award winner. In the two years before the wedding, Grace Kelly had also become a fashion icon; she was listed on numerous best-dressed lists, upheld as the paragon of classic American style, and hailed as the inspiration for what became known as the Grace Kelly Look.

On June 4, 1956, a month and a half after the wedding in Monaco, hundreds of people gathered in the bride's hometown as her wedding dress and accessories were unveiled at the Philadelphia Museum of Art; they entered the collection as a gift from the bride, Her Serene Highness Princess Grace of Monaco. In the following months and years, thousands visited the Museum to see the famous bridal gown on display, first in the Museum's Fashion Wing and later in special displays and exhibitions.

The five decades after the marriage ceremony in Monaco have confirmed Grace Kelly's wedding dress as one of the most popular and beloved objects in the Museum's collection as well as one of the most elegant and best-remembered bridal gowns of all time. The lace, pearl, and silk bridal ensemble—from the delicate cap and tulle veil to the prayer book and pumps—suited the beautiful and stylish star and was the ultimate expression of Grace Kelly's trademark look.

Princess Grace's Wedding Dress

Designed by Helen Rose (American, 1904–1985). Made by the wardrobe department of MGM, Culver City, California (founded 1924). 1956. Rose point lace, silk faille, seed pearls. Gift of Her Serene Highness, the Princesse Grace de Monaco, 1956-51-1a–d

The Kelly Family of Philadelphia

In 1876, the Centennial Exhibition in Philadelphia's Fairmount Park attracted ten million visitors. Their enthusiastic response to the exhibition of arts, crafts, and industrial products provided the impetus for the founding of the Philadelphia Museum of Art, which now stands in the park. Around that same year, John Henry Kelly and his wife, Mary Costello Kelly, both immigrants from Ireland whose families had come from County Mayo, moved from Vermont to Pennsylvania with their two small children. The Kelly family settled in the East Falls section of Philadelphia and grew to include ten children.

The couple's eighth child, John Brendan Kelly, was born in 1889. Like his parents and siblings, he went to work at an early age and proved to be quite ambitious. After laboring in his brothers' construction companies and serving in France during World War I, he started his own firm, Kelly for Brickwork, in 1919. He also worked hard to become a superb athlete, spending countless hours rowing on the Schuylkill River. Although he was restricted from competing in England's 1919 Henley Regatta, John B. Kelly went on to win two Olympic gold medals in sculling in 1920 and another in 1924. In 1924, he

Photographed around 1935 near their beach house on the New Jersey shore, the Kelly family included (from left to right) John B. Kelly, one of the world's great oarsmen and a self-made millionaire; Margaret Majer Kelly, a former physical education teacher; and children Peggy, Kell, Grace, and Lizanne. In a family of athletic extroverts, Grace was different—a reserved child who, her mother later recalled, would make up little plays with her dolls. Grace Kelly was said, however, to forget her shyness on stage and to have inherited her parents' drive and discipline.

married Margaret Majer, who was born in 1899 to a German Lutheran family. The new Mrs. Kelly, who converted to Catholicism on her marriage, was also an athlete; the recipient of a degree in physical education from Temple University, she was the first woman to teach that subject at the University of Pennsylvania. In East Falls, the couple made their home on Henry Avenue in a large house built of Kelly brick, and they instilled the virtues of hard work, thrift, and self-reliance into their children—Margaret (Peggy), born 1925; John, Jr. (Kell), born 1927; Grace, born 1929; and Elizabeth Anne (Lizanne), born 1933.

The Kelly business grew to be the one of the largest construction companies on the East Coast, and John B. Kelly became involved in local politics and civic concerns. After a narrow defeat as the Democratic candidate for mayor of Philadelphia in 1935, he was head of Philadelphia's Democratic Committee for several years. From 1938 on, he also served on the Fairmount Park Commission, which manages one of the largest civic parks in the world. The Kelly family enjoyed a prosperous life in Philadelphia, summered at their beachfront house in Ocean City, New Jersey, and regularly attended Saint Bridget's Roman Catholic Church in East Falls. Three of the Kelly children excelled at sports; indeed, Kell, coached by his father, became a champion sculler, vindicating his father by winning medals at Henley in 1947 and 1949. Grace Kelly, however, was a somewhat sickly and shy child and developed different ambitions.

Grace Kelly, Actress

Grace Kelly's mother had modeled occasionally, but it was a roommate at the Barbizon in New York who persuaded Grace Kelly to sign with an agency in her student days at the American Academy of Dramatic Arts. Although one photographer complained that she had "no oomph, no cheesecake," the young Grace Kelly's girl-next-door beauty was used to sell all types of products. Her image promoted typewriters, beer, bug spray, cigarettes, and clothing, such as this sweater she shows off in 1947 or 1948.

While John B. Kelly had been a great business success, some of his siblings had found careers in the very different world of theater. His much older brother Walter, who died in 1938, had had a successful vaudeville career performing a one-man skit, *The Virginia Judge*, while his sister Grace, after whom he had named his daughter, had been an aspiring actress before her untimely death. Another brother, George, had written a number of critically acclaimed plays in the 1920s and won a Pulitzer Prize for *Craig's Wife* in 1926. Although George Kelly had left New York to rewrite scripts in Hollywood, he communicated his enthusiasm for the theater to young Grace Kelly. Exposure to amateur acting in pageants at the convent school Ravenhill Academy, in productions at the private Stevens School, and in plays at Philadelphia's Old Academy Players Theatre increased her desire to be an actress. In 1947, she convinced her parents to let her go to the American Academy of Dramatic Arts in New York, where she studied acting for two years.

During her time as a student and fledgling actress, Grace Kelly's wholesome beauty enabled her to achieve some measure of financial independence as a model selling numerous products in ads and appearing on magazine covers. After graduating in 1949, she landed a part in August Strindberg's play *The Father*, which ran for three months on Broadway and starred Raymond Massey. She auditioned for many other parts but found her height a handicap. Miss Kelly later recalled: "Everybody said I was too tall. I've read parts in my stocking feet in the offices of every play producer in New York. I couldn't get to first base because I was 5 feet 6 1/2 [inches tall]." In 1950, she went to Hollywood for her first movie role, a young woman contemplating divorce in the film *Fourteen Hours*, released by Twentieth Century Fox in 1951. She also did summer stock at the Bucks County Playhouse in New Hope, Pennsylvania, and at Elitch's Garden Theatre in Denver. In late 1951, she again headed to California to film United Artists' western *High Noon*, in which she played the young Quaker bride of Gary Cooper's stoic marshal. While she was beautiful and suitably demure in the vaguely Victorian dress and bonnet by costume designer Ann Peck, Miss Kelly's acting did not excite the critics or live up to her own high expectations.

Back in New York, Grace Kelly took private acting lessons, appeared in numerous television plays, and auditioned for stage roles. She became known for her personal drive, combining determination and hard work to pursue her dream of becoming a serious actress. Although she made a screen test for the film *Taxi* in the spring of 1952, her goal continued to be a theater career, and she turned down contract offers from movie studios.

In the fall of 1952, however, when Grace Kelly was offered a part in the film *Mogambo*, the chance to work with John Ford and Clark Gable while getting a free trip to Africa proved irresistible. Although

she insisted on terms that would allow her to continue her stage career, the twenty-two-year-old Grace Kelly signed a seven-year contract with MGM. By signing with MGM, she became part of a powerful studio system. On a vast lot in Culver City and wherever they filmed on location, all three thousand employees worked to make MGM the greatest studio with the most successful and visually stunning films. The on-screen image of the young actress would henceforth be polished by directors, lighting designers, hairdressers, makeup artists, and costume designers.

Grace Kelly's first MGM picture was the love triangle of *Mogambo*, with Clark Gable as a big-game hunter dallying with Ava Gardner's irrepressible showgirl character, while Miss Kelly played a reserved English wife who also becomes involved with Gable. The costumes for the film were by MGM's chief designer, Helen Rose, but, although Grace Kelly would later remember the fun they had choosing clothes for the three months on location in Africa, the safari-style wardrobe gave Miss Rose little opportunity to design feminine, glamorous outfits. Released in October 1953, the film was a box-office hit that brought attention to the young newcomer and garnered her a surprise nomination for an Academy Award for best supporting actress.

MGM was at a loss as to how to next cast their new actress, who had meanwhile returned to stage acting, performing at Philadelphia's Playhouse in the Park and at various venues on Broadway. In the late summer of 1953, she was lent to Warner Brothers for Alfred Hitchcock's *Dial M for Murder*. Once again, Grace Kelly portrayed an English wife in love with someone else, but this on-screen husband, played by Ray Milland, concocts an elaborate plot to murder her. Except for a red lace dress designed by Warner's Moss Mabry, her character's clothing was bought off-the-rack. Perfectionist director Hitchcock, entranced by what he called Grace Kelly's "sexual elegance," closely supervised her look and wardrobe to ensure that her clothes went from bright to somber as her character changed. One costume suggestion from Grace Kelly was adopted, however; practical about clothes and insistent on what was right for her character, the actress told Hitchcock that her character would not don a velvet robe to answer the telephone. The director finally agreed that playing the attempted murder scene in her nightgown was better. The actress added: "After this I had his confidence as far as wardrobe was concerned. He gave me a great deal of liberty in what I would wear in the next two pictures for him, and when he brought in Edith Head to design the clothes, she and I worked together wonderfully well."

Hitchcock quickly cast Miss Kelly again in his Paramount film *Rear Window*, shot in late 1953. As the romantic interest of Jimmy Stewart's character, a photographer whose broken leg confines him to his apartment and who comes to suspect his neighbor has committed murder, Grace Kelly played a woman very much in love; the role called for understated acting that showed inner passion. Her character, a fashion model who "never wears the same dress twice," sports an extremely stylish wardrobe by Paramount's chief costume designer, Edith Head. Hitchcock, who told the designer he wanted Miss Kelly to resemble Dresden china, used her clothes to advance the conflict and action of the film. Miss Head recalled: "There was a reason for every color, every style, and he was absolutely certain about everything he settled on. For one scene, he saw her in pale green, for another in white chiffon, for another in gold. He was really putting a dream together in the studio." Glamorous short evening dresses, an impeccably tailored suit, a sheer negligee over a sleek nightgown, a full-skirted floral dress, and casual jeans all helped establish the beauty, desirability, and dimensions of the character, showing the audience what Edith Head had discovered: Grace Kelly knew how to wear clothes. Miss Head later stated, "Few actresses could have carried off the look the way Grace did." The two of them even conspired to resist Hitchcock's directive that Miss Kelly add "something" to her bosom under the nightgown.

After *Rear Window*, Paramount borrowed Grace Kelly in early 1954 to play William Holden's wife in *The Bridges at Toko-Ri*, which was based on James Michener's story of American Navy jet fighters in Asia. The costume designer was again Edith Head, who always found Grace Kelly a delight to work with; the two had even become good friends. However, as the designer later put it, this was not a costume picture. The upper middle–class apparel was relatively unexciting, and, according to one journalist, "The Kelly flavoring was just plain vanilla."

Paramount requested Grace Kelly yet again in 1954 for the role of the dowdy wife of an alcoholic actor, portrayed by Bing Crosby, in *The Country Girl*. The part demanded real acting ability, and Grace Kelly, along with many other major stars, wanted it desperately. After extensive negotiations and an agreement to make an uninteresting MGM picture, Miss Kelly was lent to Paramount for a much-inflated fee in light of her success. She was again dressed by Edith Head, and the actress and designer worked together to transform the young, beautiful star into a woman who had been married for years and lost interest in her clothes, herself, and almost everything else. While fashionably dressed in a flashback and at the end, Miss Kelly wears unflattering housedresses and shapeless cardigans for most of the film. These drab costumes were right for the part; according to Edith Head, once Grace Kelly looked truly

Above: In late 1952, Grace Kelly signed with MGM to make the film Mogambo *with Clark Gable and director John Ford. Cast as part of a love triangle, she was promoted as "an interesting blonde named Grace Kelly." Although the film was her first in Technicolor, her wardrobe was anything but colorful. Released in October 1953,* Mogambo *marked the start of Grace Kelly's rapid rise in Hollywood. Columnist Walter Winchell called this role the actress's "ticket to Stardustown."*

Opposite: Grace Kelly in one of Edith Head's designs for Rear Window, *filmed in late 1953. The pale green suit with fashionably unfitted jacket and slim skirt, worn with white blouse, belt, hat with veil, and gloves, was perfect for her role as a career woman who was "glamorous, beautiful, chi-chi, an exemplar of New York's high style." The actress's clothes also played a vital role in advancing the plot within the confined set and detailed her character. Removing her suit jacket, for example, reveals her high-necked blouse to be a shoulder-baring halter top.*

Grace Kelly wanted the challenging role of the bitter, numb-hearted wife of a cunning alcoholic in The Country Girl. At first, MGM executives refused to lend her to Paramount, but she reportedly stated: "If I can't do this picture, I'll get on a train and never come back. I'll never make another film." Miss Kelly's acting in the 1954 film was called poised and self-assured, and it brought her widespread acclaim and numerous awards. One critic noted how her "flatness of voice, lack-luster eyes, bent shoulders, and chip-on-the-shoulder manner" turned her from a lovely woman into somewhat of a shrew, a transformation helped by the drab and dowdy wardrobe created by Edith Head.

depressed, she could concentrate on her acting, which received general acclaim.

Immediately after *The Country Girl* was finished in late April 1954, Grace Kelly flew to Colombia to film MGM's potboiler *Green Fire*, starring Stewart Granger. The plot about emerald hunting in the jungles of South America once again did not give costume designer Helen Rose much scope. As a final indignity, when the film was released, some of MGM's publicity featured Miss Kelly's head pasted onto a bosomy body in a strapless green dress. "It makes me so mad," said the star. "The dress isn't even in the picture."

Alfred Hitchcock requested Miss Kelly once more for his Paramount film *To Catch a Thief*, but it was extremely doubtful MGM would lend their increasingly valuable star for a fifth time in eight months. The actress, however, assured Edith Head: "Keep right on making my clothes for the picture. I'll be in it." While finishing studio work on *Green Fire*, she went to Paramount's lot at night for costume fittings. Immediately after she wrapped *Green Fire* in the early summer of 1954, Grace Kelly went to the French Riviera to start work on Hitchcock's film. *To Catch a Thief*'s beautiful costumes and glamorous Côte d'Azur settings play almost as great a role as the plot, which concerns Cary Grant's character, a former cat burglar, who is forced to find the thief who is imitating him. In her role as a rich, spoiled American heiress, Grace Kelly was dressed in fabulous clothes and jewels; even the extras were meticulously dressed. Edith Head said Hitchcock had instructed her to make the costumes live up to the French setting, "where style is created." Paramount even sent the designer on location, which gave her and Miss Kelly the opportunity to go shopping for accessories in Paris. At Hermès, they, "like two girls in an ice-cream shop," bought so many gloves the star had to get more money. ("Gloves and shoes are the only things where Grace loses count of money," said Miss Head.) In *To Catch a Thief*, Grace Kelly's temptress character wears luxurious and alluring clothes, from a striking black-and-white beach costume to a chiffon evening dress. The denouement occurs during a spectacular masquerade ball, the most expensive costume setup Miss Head had ever done. Following Hitchcock's direction to make Grace Kelly look like a princess, she covered the actress in gold, from a curled wig to a strapless, hooped lamé dress and long gloves. Edith Head was nominated for an Academy Award for the picture, which became the designer's all-time favorite film.

In April 1954, *Life* put Grace Kelly on their cover and boldly predicted that 1954 would become "this year of Grace." By the end of that year, four of her films had been released (*Dial M for Murder* in late May, *Rear Window* in August, and both *Green Fire* and *The Country Girl* in December), while two others (*The Bridges at Toko-Ri* and *To Catch a Thief*) had been finished but not yet released. The second half of 1954 brought "a tidal wave of publicity" about Grace Kelly's sudden rise to movie stardom; she was heralded as "the latest star to reach Hollywood's top rung" and "the most outstanding new star and hottest property of the year." While her talent and intense dedication were much discussed, studio publicity had inevitably transformed her into "a Main Line debutante," even though she was not from this prestigious area of suburban Philadelphia or from the social elite. Many noted that, along with Audrey Hepburn, she represented a new type of actress, one who had obvious talent and did not depend on "artificiality to boost her stock." Miss Kelly's reserved manner differed from that of most publicity-hungry stars; she did not open her private life to the press and "flatly refused to divulge even the standard data (bust, waist, hips)." The actress's elusiveness—"writing about her," said one perceptive journalist, "is like trying to wrap up 115 pounds of smoke"—made her seem aloof, and descriptions of her cool beauty, patrician air, and "stainless steel insides" became proverbial in magazines and newspapers. *Newsweek*

Alfred Hitchcock and Grace Kelly, working together for a third time, are shown during To Catch a Thief*'s final filming sessions in Hollywood in August 1954. Miss Kelly wears Edith Head's luscious, all-gold ensemble for the elaborate costume ball that capped the picture. In what was called "a triumph of perfect casting," the actress played a lovely, self-assured rich girl; when the film was released in September of 1955, Grace Kelly was hailed as "one of the most gorgeous creatures ever to be projected upon a theater screen," who, surprisingly, could also act. This role gave Miss Kelly the chance to prove her versatility, a quality that came as no surprise to Hitchcock, who said: "She'll be different in every movie she makes. Not because of makeup or clothes but because she plays a character from the inside out. There's no one else like her in Hollywood."*

explained her appeal by saying, "Perhaps atomic-age audiences feel some vicarious reassurance and stability in watching her restrained behavior and gazing into the cool stream of the Kelly face."

Grace Kelly entered 1955 to immense acclaim, receiving the New York Film Critics Award for best actress of 1954 in January. Not everyone was completely pleased with the actress, however. Although she made *Green Fire* in order to do *The Country Girl*, she typically refused MGM's offers of parts that she felt were not right for her. She had turned down the lead in a big-budget historical extravaganza, saying that while the men duel and fight: "All I'd do would be to wear thirty-five different costumes, look pretty and frightened. . . . I just thought I'd be so bored." Given her rejection of a number of scripts, MGM reluctantly put her on suspension in early March 1955.

The studio's position was made especially difficult when Grace Kelly was nominated in mid-February, as expected, for an Academy Award for best actress for *The Country Girl*; later that month she won the Hollywood Foreign Press Association's Golden Globe Award for the role. While Judy Garland was a strong Academy Award contender for her role in *A Star is Born*, Miss Kelly's performance had earned her such praise that she was given fifty-fifty odds. On March 30, 1955, with her studio suspension lifted on a pretext, Grace Kelly went to the ceremony at Pantages Theatre wearing a dramatic ice blue satin dress and matching evening coat by Edith Head. After her name was announced as the winner, she tearfully gave her simple thanks, noting that the thrill of the moment prevented her from saying what she really felt.

In the spring and summer of 1955, the actress finally got some rest. She attended the Cannes Film Festival in May and began work on *The Swan* that fall. Grace Kelly, who received lead billing in the film, played a young "Ruritanian" princess who is courted by a crown prince (Alec Guinness) and a handsome tutor (Louis Jourdan) and learns to put duty before love. Set around 1910, the story was a costume designer's delight. Helen Rose, given the rare opportunity to design period costumes, said: "There were costumes in every conceivable situation—riding habit, fencing costume, negligees, afternoon frocks, and ball gowns. I went to work with gusto!" She used beautiful fabrics, and reported that Grace Kelly was especially thrilled with the white chiffon ball gown that had been exactingly hand embroidered with camellias by MGM's wardrobe department. Miss Rose later declared *The Swan* to be one of her best jobs and favorite assignments. While the film was not released until the following spring, reports circulated that Miss Kelly looked "like an angel" in the narrow, high-waisted dresses and soft hairstyle; these styles soon started a *Swan*-inspired fashion trend.

On December 29, 1955, Grace Kelly, back on the East Coast after filming *The Swan*, was named the highest-earning female star of the year, ranking second overall only to Jimmy Stewart—not bad for the only newcomer on the annual list. As a veteran of ten films, the recipient of an Academy Award, other honors, and critical acclaim, the actress was at the top of her professional career.

Grace Kelly's Style

By mid-1954, Grace Kelly, beautifully dressed and groomed in her on-screen roles, was becoming a familiar image off screen. Photographs of her appeared in numerous periodicals and newspapers; articles discussed her film roles but also delineated her beauty, character, and style. While the press had a field day linking her name romantically to her co-stars and other men, they generally agreed that Grace Kelly was something startlingly different from shapely but interchangeable "sweater girls" and voluptuous screen sirens such as Marilyn Monroe and Gina Lollabrigida.

The actress's personal style reflected her upbringing and ambitions. "Grace wanted to be considered serious. A consuming interest in apparel was not, in her eyes, the hallmark of a serious person," recalled Oleg Cassini, her on-and-off romantic interest in late 1954 and 1955. She was the antithesis of the showy starlet. She wore sensible and sedate clothing—shirtwaist dresses, understated evening gowns, well-cut tweed suits, hats with little veils, and low-heeled shoes—and made no secret of the horn-rimmed spectacles she needed for nearsightedness. Oleg Cassini called this her "Bryn Mawr look," and others referred to it as that of "a dream schoolmistress." Grace Kelly's tasteful style, a rarity in a young Hollywood star, appealed to many in the 1950s, when great emphasis was placed on proper feminine behavior, good grooming, and the cultivation of a pleasing appearance. When *Time* placed the

actress on its cover at the end of January 1955 with the line, "Gentlemen prefer ladies," it was neither the first nor last time this sobriquet was applied. The actress, however, was puzzled by all the talk about her being so ladylike. "I don't think I'm THAT different," she said. "I sometimes think they talk about that because there's not much happening to me." Nevertheless, in March 1955, a writer for *Vogue* noted, "Miss Kelly, in the course of her two years as a Hollywood throb, has caused dozens of writers dozens of uncomfortable moments scrounging for variations of the one phrase that pegs her—'a lady.'"

One particular clothing accessory was singled out as perhaps the most distinctive feature of the young actress's "unshow-businesslike quality." In an attempt to distill Grace Kelly's character into five words, *Time*'s article bore the headline, "The Girl in White Gloves." Miss Kelly's preference for white gloves reflected her proper upbringing; such arbiters as Emily Post decreed that women should always wear gloves in church, on city streets, in a restaurant or theater, and to go to lunch, a formal dinner, or a dance. White gloves, prim and noticeable, were worn by other well-bred girls and women of the day, but they were not common in Hollywood studios. Film director Fred Zinnemann recalled the day in 1951 when she walked into his office: "Nobody came to see me before wearing white gloves."

The young actress's appearance was not only correct but attractive. Although she did admit she had to diet now and then, Grace Kelly's height was coupled with a slender figure—she took a size 10 dress, then usually the smallest size sold—and her posture earned particular praise. Indeed, Edith Head once listed it

as the actress's best feature. With these assets, it was said she could look elegant "even in a skirt and an oversized sweater." While proper, her dress sense was also perceptive; in 1955, Miss Head named Grace Kelly as one of only five movie stars she would trust in front of a mirror as judges of their own clothes. Praise also came from Helen Rose, who said, "She has a great eye and great style; you know she will wear anything beautifully."

By late 1954, Grace Kelly's assured but understated style was publicly recognized when she was named to that year's Best-Dressed List. Started in 1940 by fashion publicist and arbiter Eleanor Lambert, who modeled it after an earlier Parisian list, this ranking of ten prominent well-dressed women began as a publicity stunt to promote the New York Dress Institute. By the mid-1950s, the Best-Dressed List had become both an annual news story and a respected barometer of style. Grace Kelly's debut occurred at a time when those named were still ranked in order; Miss Kelly was at the bottom, tied with Queen Frederica of Greece, while Mrs. William Paley and the duchess of Windsor tied for top honors.

As Grace Kelly's career blossomed throughout 1955, she also cemented her place as the quintessential example of high personal standards in dress. That spring, she was named to the seventh annual list of America's "Ten Best-Tailored Women" by the Custom Tailors Guild of America. In September, in recognition of "her personal taste, elegance, and restraint in her personal clothing," she received a Neiman-Marcus Award for distinguished service in the field of fashion and traveled to Dallas to accept it from Stanley Marcus. Grace Kelly's influence was so strong it affected others in Hollywood; one commentator noted, "Ever since she came along other stars have gone all out trying to achieve that look of stylish simplicity."

In early December 1955, the retailing organ *Women's Wear Daily* ran a feature alerting those in the clothing business to the promotional opportunities offered by something new—the Grace Kelly Look. The short article hailed the appearance of the actress with "a fresh type of natural glamour that personifies a typically American look." Miss Kelly was praised for her ability to combine a well-scrubbed appearance with elegance and always appear fashionably dressed but never overdressed. According to the newspaper, she "provides an excellent fashion model for teenagers, as she illustrates how to be casual without flying shirttails, how to be formal without looking bizarre."

The *Women's Wear Daily* article also noted that motion pictures played a dual role in molding the American ideal by both shaping and reflecting current tastes. Enthusiasm about Grace Kelly was said to be "an indication of greater maturity both in motion pictures and in public standards," since it shows "an appeal that is not based on too blatant curves, too tight dresses, too lavish furs, or jewelry noteworthy only for its abundance." Instead, the Grace Kelly Look brought attention to "the clothes and type of dressing that have long been taken for granted, and have developed almost a classic quality, exemplified by the easy shirtwaist dress, the carefully detailed tweed suit, the chiffon evening dress. Certainly, it is the way many American women like to look. Endorsement of this type of fashion by a prominent person-ality, and a movie star at that, gives it special prominence."

Soon the stylish image of Grace Kelly was everywhere, including department store windows. In the fall of 1955, her likeness was used to create a line of mannequins. Sculptor Kay Sullivan, a former Philadelphian who had studied at the Pennsylvania Academy of the Fine Arts, made a model of Miss Kelly's face for Mary Brosnan Studios of New York, the leading American designer of mannequins, which sold to stores throughout the United States and Europe.

In late December 1955, Grace Kelly was chosen "tops in entertainment" by the Associated Press. While the announcement noted her professional achievements, it emphasized the actress's effect on fashion: "So great has been her impact on the American public that she has started a whole new trend in the standard of film beauty and has influenced many of this year's collections, all of which stress the fresh young American look. Grace Kelly, a nice girl from a nice family, has made good taste glamorous."

After filming To Catch a Thief *on the French Riviera in early summer of 1954, Grace Kelly returned to New York on the* Queen Mary *with the rest of the cast and crew. Photographed on board, the beaming actress displays the sense of fun that helped make her, according to* Vogue, *"too wholesome to be mysterious." She wears a demure ensemble of a slim sheath topped by a jacket "crisped" for warm weather by a detachable white collar and cuffs. The actress was so closely associated with short white gloves that a report about the December 1955 Audience Awards said readers could gauge the evening's elegance because "Grace Kelly changed from short gloves to longies."*

Arbiters of style declared that Grace Kelly understood clothes and knew how to wear them both on and off screen; they hailed the star as the embodiment of the classic, unaffected American look that had previously been taken for granted. Oleg Cassini, for example, credited Miss Kelly with "a subdued eastern flair," noting, "By wearing clothes that don't get too much notice, she gets noticed more herself." As this publicity photograph from Rear Window *shows, her beauty and poise made even the most casual clothes look elegant.*

At the same time, the actress was named on a list of the best-tailored women in motion pictures. And, a few days later, she was selected for the 1955 Best-Dressed List. This year, however, the tally of the votes of more than a thousand fashion editors and other experts placed her not at the bottom but at the top of the list. In what was called "an almost unprecedented rise," she tied for first place with the perennial favorite Babe Cushing Mortimer Paley. Mrs. Paley was said to buy most of her wardrobe from Mainbocher, one of the world's most expensive dressmakers; she typified those who appeared on the list in the 1940s and early 1950s, who included royalty, socialites and heiresses, established actresses, influential women, and those married to men of power, influence, and wealth.

Miss Kelly's wardrobe was obviously very different from Mrs. Paley's. When asked to comment about her elevation to the top of this famous list, she said she was delighted but surprised at being selected, "I just buy clothes when they take my eye, and I wear them for years." She remarked that she still had clothes she had worn in school, and, "I wear suits quite a bit, but I also have a lot of evening gowns because of my work." When reporters wanted to know how many clothes she had, she laughingly explained that she had clothes in New York, Los Angeles, and Philadelphia, "Besides, I just buy ready-made size 10's wherever I happen to be, so I can't really tell you just what my wardrobe contains."

The two women at the top of the list, while they differed greatly in age and social roles, were tall and slender and were seen to have other similarities: While one bought couture and the other off-the-rack, both were said to "prefer simple clothes." As Edrie van Dorne noted in the *Philadelphia Inquirer*, "In choosing Miss Kelly and Mrs. Paley as current fashion leaders, the American fashion press has endorsed by implication the simplicity of the shirtwaist dress, the casual but careful costume, well-bred elegance rather than startling effect as its own ideal."

The Engagement

As 1956 began, twenty-six-year-old Grace Kelly, who had established her position at the top of her profession in a remarkably short time, had done the same in the field of fashion. It was in this climate that on January 5, 1956, the actress announced her engagement to Prince Rainier of Monaco. An official announcement was made by the couple at a small luncheon at the Philadelphia Country Club; although it was meant to be simultaneous with the Monégasque announcement, the time difference between the countries was not taken into account. International bulletins alerted the press, and when the couple returned to the Kelly family house in East Falls, it was already swarming with more than a hundred reporters and photographers. *The New York Times* described the scene as the kind "that only the television–tape recorder–color film–mass interview era can produce." During the ensuing two-hour press conference, the future bride's parents and newly betrothed couple patiently answered questions and obligingly posed for photographs, although Miss Kelly and the prince refused to kiss.

The news of her marriage came as a complete surprise to the actress's friends and fans. Newspapers across the United States and Europe splashed the story across their front pages and reported that Hollywood was flabbergasted by "the biggest bombshell to hit the town since Marilyn left Joe." Grace Kelly, "queen of Hollywood's Never-Never Land," was to marry "her true-life prince," Rainier Louis Henri Maxence Bertrand Grimaldi, the sovereign of the smallest secular state in the world. (In an indication of the lack of the prospective groom's celebrity, Philadelphia's *Evening Bulletin* included a small article entitled "His Highness's Name Is Pronounced Raynyay.")

While relatively unknown to the American public, Prince Rainier was considered to be one of the world's most eligible bachelors. Born in 1923, he had been educated in England and France, served with the Free French Forces during the Second World War, and become reigning prince of Monaco in 1949, when his mother's father had abdicated in his favor. In addition to running his principality, Prince Rainier was an avid yachtsman and scuba diver. At age thirty-two, he was called "athletically built," sometimes described as handsome, and at 5 feet 6 inches tall, slightly shorter than Miss Kelly. He was also Catholic and in need of a wife and heirs to prevent Monaco from reverting to France.

In 1297, François Grimaldi, disguised as a monk, captured the Genoese fortress of Monaco from rivals; apart from two short breaks, Monaco has been ruled by the Grimaldi family since, making them Europe's oldest ruling family. However, Monégasque history was turbulent for centuries as Spain, France, and the Italian states sought control. In 1861, Monaco's sovereignty was recognized by the Franco-Monégasque Treaty; during this same period, with the opening of the Monte Carlo Casino and the abolishment of all taxes, the principality attracted visitors and residents. In 1918, another treaty provided for limited French protection over Monaco. By 1956, although the postwar economy had dimmed its luster, residents numbered some twenty thousand (twenty-five hundred of those were Monégasque subjects).

The actress and prince had a whirlwind romance. They had met in May of the previous year, when the actress was in France for the Cannes Film Festival; at the time, she was romantically linked to dashing French actor Jean-Pierre Aumont. A French magazine, *Paris Match*, arranged for Miss Kelly to tour the palace at Monaco for a photo shoot. At her hotel that morning, the actress had been forced to cope with an electricity strike; unable to dry and style her hair or iron a dress, she and an assistant had improvised a pulled-back coiffure decorated with flowers, and she had donned her only unwrinkled outfit, a garment her friend Judy Kanter jokingly called the "dreaded taffeta dress." The dress's overwhelming floral pattern and fussy, low-waisted cut were very different from Miss Kelly's usual sleek, understated ensembles. At the palace, she met the prince, who showed her the state apartments, the museum, and his private zoo. They did not meet again until Christmas in Philadelphia, and by the new year they had decided to get married. Once the couple's engagement was announced, photographs of their initial meeting—dubbed their "first date" by the press—were printed everywhere, and the "dreaded taffeta dress" was called "the most publicized dress of the season." It was soon revealed that the famous dress, although "Dior-inspired," was not an original haute couture creation. In fact, it had been designed for the actress by McCall Patterns and worn by her on the cover of their spring 1955 pattern

Two days after her engagement, Grace Kelly went to California to film High Society. *Here she models Helen Rose's design for her character's second wedding, a ballerina-length dress of white organdy embroidered in pink and pale green over pink taffeta worn with a large picture hat. Given the speculation about her real-life nuptial garb, the press played up the star's cinematic bridal wear, printing teasing headlines such as that of Philadelphia's* Evening Bulletin *of January 11, 1956: "Miss Kelly Dons Wedding Gown."*

book. If the dress was uncharacteristic of Miss Kelly's usual simple style, it certainly had an impact; some suggested that any girl wishing to win her own Prince Charming could make the "so easy to sew" dress with 5 yards of 35-inch fabric.

On January 6, 1956, the day after their engagement, the couple made their first public appearance at a charity ball at the Waldorf-Astoria in New York, which was themed, appropriately, "A Night in Monte Carlo." Grace Kelly wore a strapless white evening gown by Christian Dior, which was complemented by a sleek chignon, a double strand of pearls, and a huge corsage—white orchids and a single red rose—to represent the colors of Monaco. The crowd of more than a thousand was dazzled by the future princess's appearance in the royal box.

The following day, the future bride, besieged by members of the press, returned to California to start filming *High Society*. In this musical remake of *The Philadelphia Story*, Grace Kelly portrays a young woman divorced from her first husband, played by Bing Crosby, and about to remarry. For the film, Helen Rose designed "a complete daytime to evening collection of modern fashion," which included a Grecian-style bathing suit, a boudoir robe, a chiffon ball gown, and a wedding dress and large hat. Miss Kelly played a role with interesting parallels to her own life. In the movie, her character, an aloof, aristocratic, affianced beauty, deals with interloping reporters covering her upcoming wedding, laughs at her image as "Miss Frigidaire," and sports an enormous engagement ring. On the set, the actress mischievously replaced the prop paste ring with the prince's gift of a real twelve-carat diamond.

At first, Miss Kelly and her fiancé were undecided about the exact timing and the location of their wedding; the ceremony would take place sometime after Easter and in the eastern United States, possibly in Philadelphia or New York. Monégasque citizens, it was reported, were heaving sighs of relief that their ruler's marriage and eventual heir would maintain their principality's independence. By the day after the announcement, however, there were demands that the wedding be held in Monaco—not only for sentimental reasons but to boost tourism, one of the country's principal sources of income. *The Philadelphia Inquirer* retorted by pointing out that "Roman Catholic weddings usually are held in the parish of the bride, which in this case requires the services to be held in Philadelphia." Both the bride's mother and the local papers did not easily give up the struggle to have the ceremony at Saint Bridget's in East Falls, but in the end Monaco prevailed.

The Wedding Phenomenon

Interest in the "fairy-tale" romance and royal wedding was so great that late winter and spring of 1956 seemed to be dominated by media references to the famous couple. The Philadelphia press naturally devoted extensive coverage to their hometown princess-to-be, but many papers across the country were similarly occupied and issued almost daily bulletins. On January 23, it was announced that Helen Rose would design Miss Kelly's wedding dress; on February 6, the dates for the civil wedding (April 18) and the cathedral wedding (April 19) were confirmed; on February 21, the names of the wedding party were released; and, on March 12, it was announced that the Philadelphia Museum of Art would be given the dress after the wedding. Information about the nuptials continued to be released on a regular basis; in addition, almost every day brought a new flood of minutia, speculation, and rumination on the ubiquitous topic. These included the number of titles the bride would have after her marriage, the effect of marriage on her film career, the varied and numerous presents the couple received, the names on the wedding guest list, and the prince's devotion of twelve hours a day to wedding plans.

Some attempts were made to explain the excessive interest in Grace Kelly's wedding. Writing for the Hearst syndicate, political columnist George Sokolsky theorized that the preoccupation with Cold War politics might be the cause: "There is too much Russia in our lives. It must do something to the gall bladder if not the liver. Maybe that is why Grace Kelly's betrothal to Grimaldi seems so important; at any rate, it is a relief, almost an escape from the Russians." He went on to muse, "I wonder if Monaco officially is on our side, on Krushchev's side, or neutral."

With such widespread interest in the wedding, many were inclined to capitalize on its commercial potential. As columnist Elmer Roessner observed, "Almost every American merchandiser with a touch of Barnum in him is itching to tie products in with the Grace Kelly–Prince Rainier wedding." In early

March, the Kellys publicly notified merchandisers of potential legal ramifications if they tried to profit from the royal wedding. The family's lawyer placed a notice in *Women's Wear Daily*, warning that the use of the names or seals of the couple "in any manner, either directly or indirectly, for commercial purposes, or to further the sale of merchandise or items of any kind," without prior authorization, would be vigorously prosecuted.

Nonetheless, a sure way to get mentioned in the press was to have some sort of connection to the royal wedding. Max Factor announced that, at the bride's request, it would design a special cosmetic to match her wedding gown. The bride's $150 nuptial nylons, said hosiery-maker Willys de Mond of Hollywood, would be pearl-trimmed stockings specially made by the firm as a wedding gift, a claim refuted by Miss Kelly a few weeks later. The commercial frenzy even extended to the staid realm of menswear. Philadelphia's After Six Company, which supplied the men of the Kelly family and the ushers with three outfits each, publicized a new style of lapel—the Monaco—they had created for tail coats and dinner jackets in honor of the wedding.

By late March, unremitting publicity about the couple and their wedding caused the future bride to declare wearily, "The prince and I are awfully tired of reading about ourselves, and we thought other people would be also." Some members of the press and public concurred; on April Fools' Day one columnist joked about a cruise specially organized to take those onboard out of earshot of the wedding hoopla still to come. Most, however, were happy to be swept away by the celebrity-royal romance, and, in early April, it was said that, "in recent weeks, almost no newspaper went to press without at least one mention of Grace Kelly."

The Grace Kelly Look

Once her engagement was announced, the already sizable influence Grace Kelly had on fashion escalated. In mid-January, inspired by the young woman "currently making headlines around the world in realms of career, fashion, and romance," the Grace Kelly Look that *Women's Wear Daily* had described the previous month was big fashion news for spring. While Miss Kelly was said to typify the philosophy of "be yourself," it was stressed that "this look is not easy to come by, casual and unstudied though it appears. The simple, uncluttered kind of clothes she wears—and that you will be wearing this spring—demand that the wearer be groomed to the nth degree; that her hair and complexion fairly sparkle; in short be that ultimate in cool, beautiful simplicity typified by Miss K." The writer also noted: "Actually, this Kelly look isn't anything new. It's been beloved by college girls for generations. It's long been called the 'American' look. It fits in beautifully with our way of life, casual, unaffected. With such a shining example as a guide, we're sure going to look pretty this spring."

Miss Kelly's "clean-cut kind of beauty" and the Grace Kelly Look soon dominated the beauty industry, which stressed disarmingly understated makeup along with regular brushing and shampoo sessions to get "that polished, satiny gleam simply-styled hair must have." While many women asked their hairdressers to give them Grace Kelly's hairstyle, not all women looked like the actress; clever hairdressers therefore softened the look with curls or bangs.

For the spring collection of 1956, two completely different feelings and silhouettes—the T-Square Silhouette and the Grace Kelly Look—had been endorsed by fashion designers and American women, said Kittie Campbell in Philadelphia's *Sunday Bulletin* on February 26, 1956. She described the first—

The Grace Kelly Look
The T-Square Silhouette

a "slender reed of a dress" topped by a wide hat—as severe, authoritative, and dramatic. She called the graceful Kelly style "softer, younger, and, frankly, more easily worn" as well as more subtle:

It is a matter of understatement, the long line top which shows off the lithe, small waistline of a figure. The gently full skirt is unpetticoated. The hat counts its size in depth and not with width. Many of the "feminists" in fashion designers prefer this line, showing it in ensembles, dresses, and coats. . . . The interesting thing about the contrast of the opposite looks is that it reverts to the old fashion question "would you rather look pretty—or smart?"

It was not only in the United States that the influence of Grace Kelly and her upcoming wedding was felt. The style of "Philadelphia's long-stemmed blonde princess" had an effect on casual clothes on the French Riviera and on almost every aspect of fashion in France, where thanks to her, it was said simplicity and good taste were definitely back in style. Parisian designers were said to have the actress in mind while sketching their upcoming collections. French fashion houses favored blond mannequins and chose colors to flatter the fair-haired. "Bridal white" was almost the keyword for the season, and regal splendor was preferred for formal and evening wear. "Apparently la belle Kelly," commented Kittie Campbell, "has captured the imagination of the people over there no less than the romance has impressed us here at home." Modeling agencies in the United States and France were reported to be "frantically searching" for wholesome, dignified, ladylike models. One New York agency reported: "We hear Kelly, Kelly, Kelly—twenty times a day."

In March 1956, the Fashion Academy named Miss Kelly as the best-dressed actress on yet another list of the nation's best-dressed women. That month, the actress was also chosen as one of America's ten best-hatted women by the New York Millinery Council because "she brings a fragile womanly appeal to the new [large-brimmed] hats reminiscent of the turn of the century . . . and because, being Irish, she knows that a beautiful hat can beat the Irish themselves at flattery." Miss Kelly was also credited with helping to change attitudes about women wearing eyeglasses, said to have become not only acceptable but an important fashion accessory. By late March, Grace Kelly's tasteful style even influenced beachwear. Designer Fred Cole, when announcing a new bathing suit (named "Her Serene Highness") noted: "Today the ideal is the lady-like look personified by Grace Kelly. And people are discovering that 'lady-like' doesn't mean sexless. Such appeal can be on a very high frequency, like a supersonic dog whistle." By early April, when Miss Kelly sailed for Monaco, she had "come to be regarded as the epitome of good taste in dress" and was an acknowledged fashion leader, while the Grace Kelly Look was "a phrase voiced with reverence throughout the fashion world."

Grace Kelly's Trousseau

Amy Vanderbilt, in her *Complete Book of Etiquette* of 1952, wrote that the trousseau of a wealthy Victorian bride was expected to include clothing to last at least a year along with vast quantities of personal and household linen. In mid-twentieth-century America, the author continued, rapid changes of fashion and frequent moves had tempered such excess, but while assembling a trousseau was much easier, the modern well-to-do bride customarily provided household goods, dainty lingerie, and a personal wardrobe for her new life. While Miss Kelly's purchase of towels was given minor press coverage—mostly because her mother had them monogrammed in a nonroyal fashion—the clothing acquisitions of such a major figure in the fashion world were the subject of a great deal of speculation and newsprint.

In Philadelphia, fashion mavens reacted with dismay at the "chilling rumor" that the celebrated bride might fill her wedding wardrobe needs at Neiman-Marcus, which did indeed supply part of her trousseau. Kittie Campbell of Philadelphia's *Evening Bulletin* proclaimed:

Grace is our girl. She knows the Philadelphia shops. . . . Grace's mother shopped here for her rompers and cottons. . . . The Kelly girls have had many a "ball" in shopping tours through Philadelphia before the big dance or a family social occasion. . . . Philadelphians all feel like "part of the family" in this royal romance, or at least fancy themselves as "her loyal subjects." I hope

In mid-March of 1956, Grace Kelly leaves MGM's famed studio lot—the "walled city of white stucco"—in Culver City. Prince Rainier had declared that his wife would not resume film work; while the actress said she would abide by his wishes, she stated she had not asked to be released from her contract but was taking a year's leave of absence. MGM, hoping their valuable star would return, made every effort to please her. While film costumes were usually reused, they were occasionally purchased by or given to favored actresses. MGM generously (and with a fair amount of fanfare) gave Miss Kelly all of her High Society costumes. Here, Miss Kelly and her friend Rupert Allan struggle to keep the voluminous skirts off the ground. Since the film was set in Newport in the summer, Helen Rose noted that the garments would be perfect for wear on the French Riviera.

she'll treat us as "family"—and let us feel that we have part in the wedding, if not the ceremony itself, then in the fun of knowing the thrills, the dreams, the normal girl-in-love charm behind the trousseau. It isn't a commercial gesture I am talking about at all. We are all very proud of Grace Kelly, and we are also proud of the fashion shops, which can lay such treasures at her feet as belong in the dream trousseau of a princess. We would like her to "stay in the Philadelphia family."

While others were very interested in her new wardrobe, Miss Kelly was busy working on *High Society* in Hollywood. Filming was finished by mid-March, but Miss Kelly postponed her departure for New York in order to present the Academy Award for best actor on March 21. During this time, she was repeatedly quoted as saying that she had not had any time to shop for her trousseau. "I'm so far behind now in preparations that I won't even have time for last-minute details," she told the Associated Press. She left Hollywood, however, with a solid start to her bridal wardrobe. MGM gave its star the dozen Helen Rose–designed outfits from *High Society*, and Helen Rose had also thrown Grace Kelly a lingerie shower, where guests such as Betsy (Mrs. Cary) Grant, Celeste Holm, and Ann Blyth had given the bride night-gowns, peignoirs, negligees, bed-jackets, slips, and bras, many of which were trimmed with hand-embroidery and imported lace.

When she finally arrived in New York, Miss Kelly had twelve days to complete her trousseau shop-ping, visit with friends, attend the wedding of her bridesmaid Rita Gam, go to several bridal showers in her honor (including one where Alfred Hitchcock sent her a shower curtain), and spend one last Easter with her family in Philadelphia before sailing to her new home. Reports indicated that the "year's busiest bride" was in a "whirl of parties" and "up to her eyebrows in preparations."

While a full description of the wardrobe assembled by Miss Kelly was not revealed until she had sailed for Monaco, the bride's wedding preparations were nevertheless regarded as, in *Life*'s jocular phrase, "a monumental public project." As the bride-to-be "swept from one expensive store to another, following a planned timetable with clocklike precision," she was trailed by photographers and reporters who recorded every last-minute detail "for an insatiably inquisitive world." Wherever she went, from Fifth Avenue department stores to specialty shops, she immediately attracted enormous crowds, which forced her to shop early in the morning as soon as the stores opened. While in California, the clever bride had enlisted the help of her friend Eleanor Lambert, director of the New York Dress Institute and doyenne of the Best-Dressed List. The fashion arbiter's educated legwork helped the bride make the most of her limited time, and Miss Lambert's industry connections solved another difficulty—shopping for out-of-season summer clothing. Hearing of the bride's plight, designers sent box after box of samples from their upcoming collections to Miss Kelly's apartment; after she made her selections, they worked day and night to finish the orders.

Grace Kelly's shopping spree pleased many merchants and designers. Noting her innate sense of style, one commented: "Of course, it's easy to dress her. . . . She has the ideal body to build a dress on—you just can't go wrong." A number of firms were so delighted to have their creations included in her famous wardrobe that they presented the requested items to Miss Kelly as gifts. The bride's

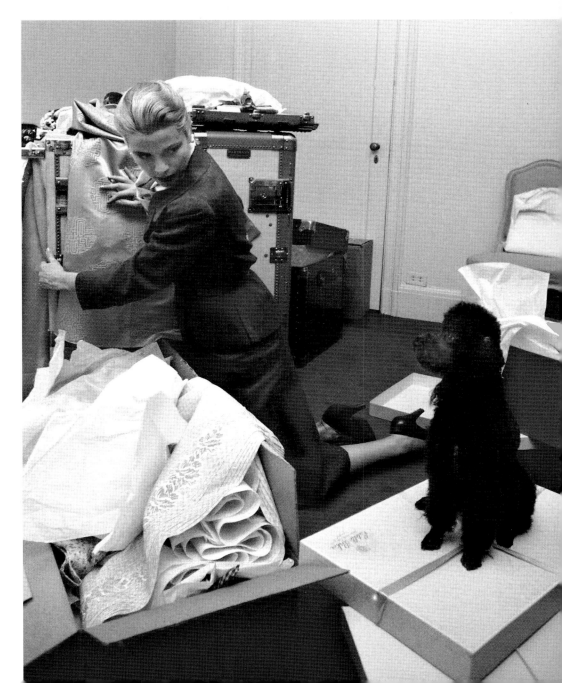

Grace Kelly in her New York apartment packing before leaving for Monaco, watched by her poodle, Oliver. This was one of the photographs that accompanied an April 9, 1956, Life *article about the famous bride's wedding preparations. Miss Kelly did all her own packing because, she said, it saved time and confusion in the long run. She included old favorites, like the brocade cheongsam (seen beneath her right hand) that she had worn in February to receive an award from the Hollywood Foreign Press Association. Her recent trousseau purchases included seven evening gowns, six cocktail dresses, sixteen day costumes, and numerous suits, coats, furs, and accessories. While bouffant gowns and ballerina-length skirts had to be packed in reams of tissue paper, it was her many new hats—more, she said, than she could possibly wear—that were the biggest packing challenge.*

patronage was widespread; while much of her shopping was done in New York, she also ordered clothes through Los Angeles stores such as I. Magnin and bought items from the Philadelphia shop Nan Duskin. One fashion writer noted, "The list of designers included in Miss Kelly's trousseau almost sounds like a 'who's who' of America [sic] design." Among the designers she patronized, Ben Zuckerman was a favorite; he was reportedly so rushed filling her order for a tweed suit and a coat that he had to delay work on his fall and winter collection. Evening dresses came from Harvey Berin and Fira Benenson; cocktail and evening dresses from Philadelphia-born James Galanos; evening clothes from Pauline Trigère and Ceil Chapman; day and cocktail clothes from Traina-Norell; cocktail outfits from Samuel Winston; day clothes from Adele Simpson, Mollie Parnis, Larry Aldrich, and Ceil Chapman; summer dresses from Suzy Perette; sports clothes from B. H. Wragge; and furs from Leo Ritter. Ever practical, the bride included a Claire McCardell cotton bathing suit and made sure she had "oodles of short[s], slacks, and sun dresses for lounging on the yachting honeymoon."

In her selection of forty outfits, Grace Kelly endorsed both short and long evening hemlines and the full-skirted and slim-line silhouettes of 1950s fashion. She favored silk for both evening and daywear and selected it in delicate colors—pink, yellow, blue, and white—that suited her blonde hair and fair complexion. Beige was one of her "important and favorite colors," and it was represented in shades of almost white to amber with names such as "French Bread" and "Flax." Miss Lambert praised the bride's "thrift, discrimination, and firm budget control," noting that she ruthlessly discarded anything that was faddish or extreme, did not fit into her color scheme, or required an inordinate amount of care.

Accessories, a major part of the ladylike look that Miss Kelly had perfected, were also carefully selected for her trousseau. She bought silk chiffon scarves, and purchased almost thirty pairs of shoes made by David Evins and Delman. Miss Kelly did not forget her headwear; indeed, she confided to intimates that she had "gone hat-happy" and bought far too many of them. Among the milliners she patronized were Lilly Daché, Don Marshall, Mr. Fred of John Frederics, who created hats to complement outfits designed by Helen Rose, and Sidney Guillaroff, the chief hair designer at MGM. Even her fiancé famously got in on the millinery act; through an intermediary, he arranged to send her a hat to wear at Easter in Philadelphia. His gift was the subject of several days of discussion in the press (would it arrive in time? the back-up was a half-hat of pink straw). Designed by Sally Victor (even the prince, it was noted, bought American!), the beige straw hat draped with matching maline net was "the center of feminine attention" when Miss Kelly, guarded by fifteen policemen and three detectives, wore it to Easter mass at Saint Bridget's.

When the *Philadelphia Inquirer* was at last able to report the full details of Grace Kelly's trousseau just before the wedding, Cynthia Cabot, the newspaper's fashion editor, stated that the bridal wardrobe was "a powerful stimulation to the garment trade," since, after reading about the trousseau, any housewife would think her own closet empty and be inspired to buy new clothes. Cabot also noted: "Even a fashion editor, accustomed as she is to seeing and describing beautiful clothes, is impressed by the luxury—and the good taste—of this trousseau. Expensive and large as it is, still this is a practical wardrobe for a girl who's going to lead the life of a princess. And in its quiet, tasteful beauty it will show the people she meets that Miss Kelly comes from a country with dress designers of great distinction, equal to any in the world."

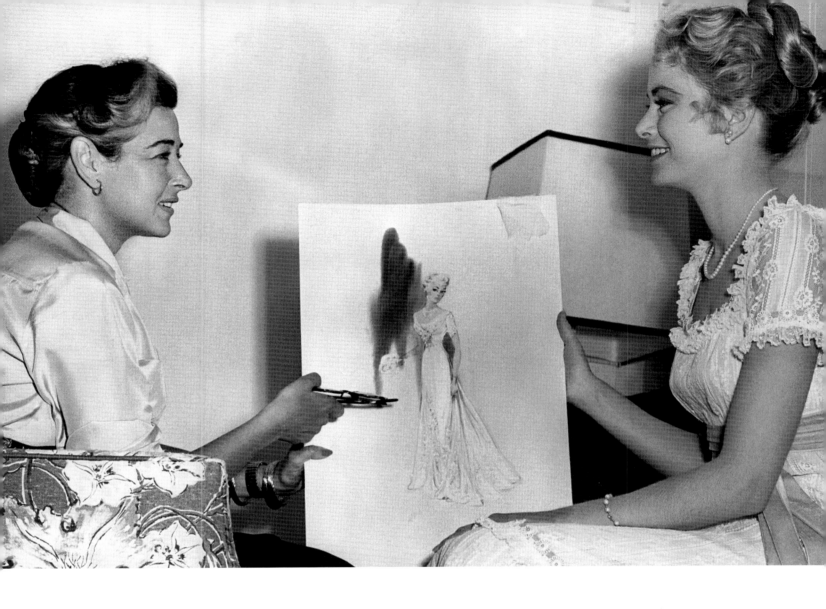

The Design and Construction of the Wedding Dress

In this publicity shot, designer Helen Rose discusses her sketch of a costume for The Swan with the film's star, Grace Kelly, who models the early-twentieth-century-style high-waisted dress and soft hairstyle that started a fashion trend even before the film's premiere. In what was seen as a fascinating coincidence, the actress played a princess in this 1955 film; the experience, it was said, gave her an education in courtly manners and such royal accomplishments as fencing and kissing "with regal restraint." Although MGM delayed releasing The Swan until April 1956 to take advantage of the wedding fervor surrounding Miss Kelly, this photograph was printed everywhere in late January 1956 after it was announced that Helen Rose would design Grace Kelly's real-life wedding dress.

While Grace Kelly's trousseau received a fair amount of attention, her wedding dress was the focus of the most ardent interest. Once her engagement to Prince Rainier was announced on January 5, 1956, Miss Kelly was immediately besieged with offers from American and European designers, stores, and couturiers to design the dress for the big day. Speculation about which designer would get the honor and the ensuing publicity was put to rest on January 23, when it was revealed that Helen Rose would design the dress, which would be a present to the bride from MGM. Miss Kelly's close friend Edith Head, costume designer at Paramount, had been among those hoping to be given the coveted design job. According to Edith Head's biographer, the designer was more than disappointed: "When it was announced that Helen Rose would design her wedding dress, Edith was livid but Kelly coolly reminded her: 'MGM is paying for it. Would Paramount do that?' Edith had to admit that Paramount wouldn't."

MGM had a precedent for giving their stars wedding gowns if they were married while under contract. This gift could be an incentive for an actress to get married and maintain her wholesome reputation, while the studio could use the occasion as publicity for their actress and designer. In the case of a valued star, the studio's largesse could be especially grand. When Elizabeth Taylor married Nicky Hilton in 1950, MGM paid for the reception and the attendants' dresses as well as the magnificent wedding gown, designed by Helen Rose. In the early 1950s, MGM stars had almost as many weddings off screen as on film; by 1956, Helen Rose had designed another personal wedding dress for Miss Taylor, as well as two for Jane Powell and one each for Ann Blyth, Arlene Dahl, Pier Angeli, and several other stars.

In the case of Grace Kelly, MGM was put in a difficult position when they were informed of her wedding plans the day before the public announcement. The actress, who still had four years remaining on her contract, was a valuable MGM asset. Studio executives were uncertain if, under the terms of her contract, they could force her to make more films, and doing so would have antagonized both the star and her fans. With two unreleased Grace Kelly films to promote and the fervent hope that she would return to make more films after her marriage, MGM was extremely accommodating; they continued to pay Miss Kelly's salary, gave her a large bonus, presented her with her costumes from *High Society*, and paid hairdresser Virginia Darcy and publicist Morgan Hudgins to accompany the star to Monaco for the wedding. Nor were the advantages of presenting a wedding dress to such an admired actress making such an acclaimed marriage lost on them. Princess Grace later recalled, "During the shooting of *High Society* the studio very kindly offered me my wedding dress and said that Helen would design it."

Costume designer Helen Rose, born in 1904 in Chicago, attended the Chicago Academy of Fine Arts and then designed costumes for vaudeville and nightclub acts. After moving to Los Angeles in 1929, she worked for a film wardrobe company and briefly for Fox Studios. She later became the Ice Follies' designer, a job she continued even after she returned to film costuming. In 1942, she was hired by Twentieth Century Fox as the costume designer for musical numbers; the following year MGM, looking for new talent after the departure of their famed chief designer, Adrian, in 1941, brought her on staff to work under their new chief designer, Irene. In the late 1940s, Irene left to open a couture business and, although Walter Plunkett costumed most of MGM's period films, Miss Rose became their main costume designer; by 1956, she had designed clothes for top stars in more than ninety films. Once Academy Awards started to be given for costume design in 1948, Helen Rose was repeatedly nominated and won the 1952 award for *The Bad and the Beautiful* and the 1955 award for *I'll Cry Tomorrow*. In the 1950s, MGM's film style continued to emphasize visual allure rather than gritty realism; Helen Rose's elegant, understated, but up-to-date designs suited Grace Kelly and MGM's style well. She designed the clothes for four of Miss Kelly's films: *Mogambo*, *Green Fire*, *The Swan*, and *High Society*.

When Helen Rose received the assignment to design Miss Kelly's wedding gown, both of them were very busy with *High Society*. They did, however, find time to have several conferences about the future princess's wedding dress. According to Helen Rose, they exchanged design ideas, and used one of the ball gowns from *High Society* as a starting point for the design, although the bride requested the addition of a long train for her cathedral wedding. Princess Grace later said, "I explained to Helen the kind of line and look I wanted, with *gros de longre* [sic] skirt and lace blouse, and, as usual, she came up with something that far surpassed my imagination and hopes." The design process left Helen Rose with a high opinion of Grace Kelly: "She is a dream to work with. . . . I showed her two sketches of the final design and she chose the one she wanted. That was all there was to it."

The design for the dress was traditional in many ways, but it could also be considered something of a departure in bridal wear. Indeed, when Helen Rose used a similar idea in 1952 for Dorothy McGuire's character in MGM's melodrama *Invitation*, she was said to have "upset style tradition by turning out something brand new in a wedding gown." The dress for the film consisted of a rose point lace blouse and a skirt that were "welded together" by a separate cummerbund. The supposed advantage of the design was that, after the marriage ceremony, the blouse could be worn with smart dinner suits and the skirt could be paired with other blouses for formal wear. An obvious precursor to Grace Kelly's bridal gown, the film's dress features a modest V neck and long sleeves, but the lace on the bodice lacks definition and the satin skirt is caught up in a dramatic knee-length pouf at the sides and back. Four years later, Helen Rose refined the idea to make a more detailed and more elegant dress for the future princess.

To create a magnificent wedding dress for Grace Kelly, MGM made available every resource of their wardrobe department, which they described as "the largest and most complete in the world." Occupying seven buildings and warehouses, it was said to have had more than a half million costumes in stock, and it operated like a full-scale garment factory with a staff of more than 150 wardrobe workers that "designs and makes costumes, both modern and period, for both men and women in all MGM pictures." The complicated costume-making process involved fabric shoppers and dyers, tailors, finishers, and pressers. Making Grace Kelly's wedding dress required the special skills of several subdepartments: women's wardrobe, which had a staff of thirty-six, including cutters and fitters, drapers, and seamstresses; the millinery department, which consisted of five professionals headed by Suzanne Hoffman, who had been brought from Paris when Adrian was MGM's head designer; and the embroidery department, which employed about fifteen skilled workers.

The studio later stated that making Grace Kelly's formal wedding gown took six weeks and involved thirty-five MGM craftspeople, including the most expert seamstresses, milliners, beaders, embroiderers, and dyers. According to Helen Rose, Grace Kelly had greatly endeared herself to the studio's wardrobe department, and they all wanted her dress to be a masterpiece. The sewing was done, Miss Rose said, by Ethel "Brucie" Ryan. There had been so many recent brides at MGM that the seamstress had previously said she could not make another wedding dress. But, Helen Rose remembered, Brucie changed her mind when the name of the bride-to-be was revealed: "When I told her I was designing the wedding dress for Gracie, what could she do? Like everyone else at the studio, she loves her, too!" With great effort and skill, the assembled team created the wedding gown, headpiece, veil, and prayer book, as well as a dress for the civil marriage ceremony.

Miss Kelly, while required for long hours on the set of *High Society*, was naturally interested in the evolution of her wedding gown. Because she was working at the studio, she was on hand for the numerous required fittings, could check samples of beading, and was able to otherwise ensure that the wedding dress would be everything she wanted for her big day.

MGM was Hollywood's largest movie studio in the mid-1950s; indeed, they claimed to be "the greatest entertainment enterprise in the history of the world." In 1955, MGM spent $55 million making 30 films, and their 3,000 employees performed 250 different types of jobs. The enormous wardrobe department was aptly described as a "beehive of activity." This photograph shows workers in women's wardrobe, where costumes were painstakingly created for "the most glamorous women in the world." Grace Kelly would later recall her wardrobe experiences as delightful: "The fitters and seamstresses at MGM were top-flight and they worked for perfection."

The actress, her fans, and vicarious romantics were not the only ones intensely interested in the design of her wedding dress. Mal Caplan, head of the MGM wardrobe department, later recalled to Helen Rose: "Every manufacturer of wedding apparel in the country wanted to get a copy of the sketch or a picture of the gown itself, or even just an impression of what you were doing. They were making all kinds of offers." Security was therefore tight: "During the making of the gown, the sketch was never left in the fitting room. The gown was locked up every evening during the making and the area was completely enclosed with partitions so that no one could even see the gown during its construction."

While the wedding dress was being made, the press relentlessly tried to pump the designer and the bride for details. In early February, Aline Mosby of Philadelphia's *Evening Bulletin* interviewed Miss Rose in MGM's "fancy fitting rooms" and discovered the gown "will not be as fancy as the public might expect." Miss Kelly wanted the dress to be traditional, with long sleeves and a high neckline, and Miss Rose thought it should reflect the actress' personality—"simple but elegant, feminine, ladylike but not necessarily regal," adding that Miss Kelly's gown should "not overpower her beauty. That is more important than trying to be regal." Miss Rose told the reporter: "The gown will be very expensive but not ornate. It will be a museum piece as far as workmanship is concerned." A week or so later, gossip columnist Louella Parsons, who had spent some time with the future bride on the set of *High Society*, revealed that the actress would wear "a bridal veil and dress of Brussells [*sic*] rose point lace at the religious ceremony" made from what was said to be "125-year-old priceless lace" obtained in Europe.

While there were these few hints about the dress, no specifics would be confirmed until two days before the wedding when details would be released by the studio; until then, plans for the wedding dress were "as closely guarded as the plans for a fifteen-hundred-mile ballistic missile." In the build-up to the royal wedding, newspaper headlines made the most of the mystery surrounding Miss Kelly's bridal attire. On March 20, the *New York Times* reported, "Designer Mum on Kelly Dress"; on April 10, the *Los Angeles Times* announced, "Grace's Bridal Gown Has Veil—of Secrecy"; on April 11, Philadelphia's *Daily News* proclaimed, "Designer Buttons Lip on Grace's Gown"; and on the same day the *Philadelphia Inquirer* did not even have to mention the bride-to-be's name in its headline: "That Bridal Gown Is Still a Secret." In numerous interviews over several months, Helen Rose—"currently the most discussed and certainly the most mysterious designer in the world"—repeatedly explained the reasons for the secrecy. She had made a pledge to the bride, who wanted her wedding gown to be a surprise. (Miss Kelly herself had smilingly told a reporter, "We can't let the prince see it before the wedding, you know.") Miss Rose said every bride she had dressed felt the same, "I'm surprised that anyone even asks about it." She also mentioned that when a previous bridal design of hers for another prominent actress had received pre-wedding publicity, widely advertised copies were in stores for $29.75 before the distressed bride could wear it.

In what was most probably an attempt to further obscure the details of the dress, the designer was quoted at the end of March as "reporting breathlessly, 'The design fell apart. We've changed the whole thing. . . . It won't be of lace after all.'" Thus in mid-April, after months of speculation, there was still "the Big Question—what kind of dress will Grace Kelly wear when she becomes Princess Grace?" In an attempt to answer this, Helen Rose's general ideas about wedding gowns were sought and analyzed. Miss Rose, it was reported, thought most wedding gowns get too busy by combining lace and organdy and ruffles. Along with simplicity, she also emphasized the importance of proper fit, noting that three-quarters of the studio's cost for a garment was for labor to ensure a perfect fit: "Everything we do is with a view to how it will photograph—and if it fits well, it photographs well." The designer endorsed big, beautiful wedding gowns with traditional long sleeves and high neck, and she noted that the back of a wedding dress should be a focal point because that is what is on view when the bride stands at the altar. Helen Rose also considered veils very important, saying: "It's probably my movie training. We have to design for close-ups that are good from the waist up!" As for color, Miss Rose said she preferred soft ivory rather than pure white.

By April 5, a few specific details of the gown's fabric had been leaked: *Women's Wear Daily* reported that, according to "reliable sources," 18 1/2 yards of off-white Italian faille taffeta would be used with the rose point lace, and that the gown would be worn with a cap and circular veil. In early April, the magazine *Motion Picture*, perhaps acting on further insider information, published a sketch depicting the royal couple in their wedding finery. While the illustration would eventually prove to be a fairly accurate representation of the wedding dress, it was swiftly and strongly repudiated by Helen Rose as inauthentic and unauthorized. The press and public may have derived some vague idea of what Grace Kelly's wedding dress would look like from these various reports, but even without specifics, there was no doubt as to the gown's importance and Grace Kelly's fashion influence. Before details of the dress were released, Cynthia Cabot considered the impact of the gown:

Because she is a kind of fairy princess to a world that adores a romance, Miss Kelly embodies the

Princess Grace's Wedding Shoes. Designed by David Evins (American, born England, 1907–1991). 1956. Rose point lace, silk faille, seed pearls, glass beads, leather. Gift of Her Serene Highness, the Princesse Grace de Monaco, 1956-51-2a,b

David Evins believed sheer simplicity was his forte, and summed up his design philosophy when he said, "It's not what you put on but what you take off." Miss Kelly's bridal shoes are classic pumps, a style for which the designer was famous, with rounded toes and 2 1/2-inch-high Louis heels. The main design feature is provided by the cordonnet, or thread, outlines around the lace motifs, which include a rosette on the vamp accented with seed pearls and clear glass beads. The left shoe is embossed inside with "Grace Kelly" in gold capital letters, while the right is embossed with "design by Evins," with his name in its trademark script.

beauty that every bride wishes were her own, and the fabric, silhouette and details of her wedding dress have a significance far beyond their own intrinsic merit. . . . We can be sure that the gown will be lovely, gracious, and dignified. For the rest we must wait.

There isn't any doubt that Miss Kelly's gown will be quickly copied, that manufacturers are standing ready with sketch pad and scissors in hand, eager to present reasonable facsimiles as fast as they can to girls wishing to imitate one of their favorite movie stars.

More important than this rather ephemeral effect, however, is still the fact that beautifully groomed and casually tailored in her everyday wardrobe, Miss Kelly has influenced for the best the working-day costume of the average American girl.

Finishing Touches

Because there were no firm details about the gown, the press welcomed news about any aspect of Grace Kelly's wedding attire. On February 27, Philadelphia's *Bulletin* announced: "First specific word on what princess-to-be Grace Kelly will wear for her April wedding to Prince Rainier of Monaco has to do with her shoes. . . . Distinguished New York shoe designer David Evins has been commissioned to design two pairs of shoes for Her Grace."

David Evins, born in 1907, came to the United States from England at age thirteen. He graduated from New York University and studied illustration at the Pratt Institute in Brooklyn. While working as a fashion illustrator for *Vogue*, Evins altered the style of some shoes he drew; when the shoe company complained, the editor fired him, saying that if Evins liked shoe designing so much, he should do it for a living. He took this advice and began working in the shoe industry, and after the Second World War he was given his own label by I. Miller. His career advanced rapidly; by the mid-1950s, he had received a

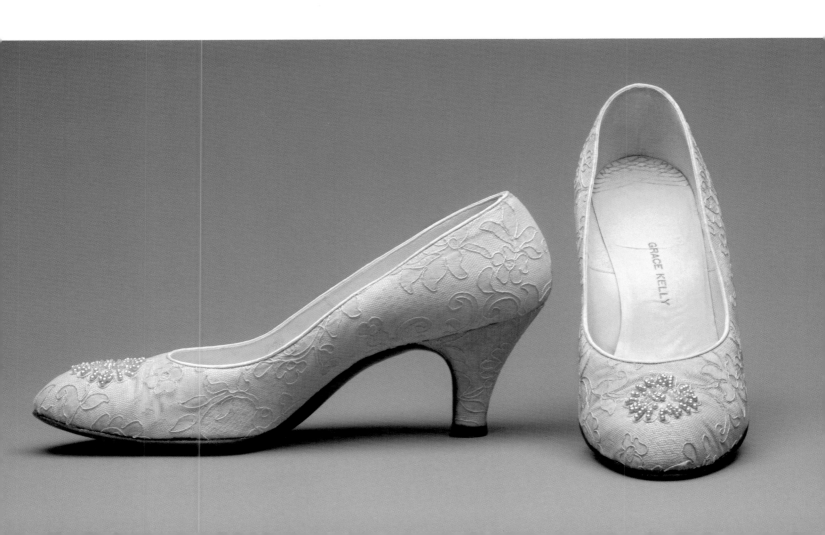

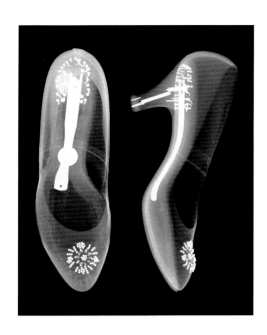

Coty American Fashion Critics' Award, achieved fame as "the King of Pumps," and became America's top shoe designer. Evins operated a factory in Europe and produced classic, understated footwear for discriminating clients, including many Broadway and Hollywood stars and productions.

Evins had made shoes for Miss Kelly for some of her movie roles and provided many pairs for her trousseau; as the premier American footwear maker, he was the natural choice to make her bridal shoes. While simple, the lace and silk shoes did involve some drama. A small piece of the precious lace matching the dress was sent to Evins from Hollywood, but it tore when stretched over the last. Knowing that there was no more of the original lace to spare, a frantic Evins dispatched his wife, Marilyn, to search New York for matching antique lace. Told that money was no object in this emergency, she had to pay a shockingly high sum to a dealer for a few square inches of suitable lace.

Miss Kelly's wedding shoes—or more precisely their heels—were also mentioned by some who wished to belittle the groom. On March 1, gossip columnist Walter Winchell acerbically commented: "David Evins is making Grace's wedding shoes. Low heels. So His Serene Highness won't look like a shrimp at the altar." Although the idea that Miss Kelly wore flats or very low heels is firmly entrenched and still repeated, the shoes are classic pumps with 2 1/2-inch-high heels.

Grace Kelly's bridal shoes do contain one secret, however. Philadelphia's *Bulletin* revealed that "with an appreciation for superstitions and omens that bespeaks her Irish ancestry, Grace has requested that the traditional copper penny for good luck be hidden in the construction of the shoes." In various times and places, the lucky object in a bride's shoe could be a piece of silver, a sixpence, a penny, or a dime. In mid-twentieth-century America, most brides simply put a coin inside one of their shoes—a bride "must at least pay discomfort for her 'luck,'" remarked Emily Post—but in Miss Kelly's custom-made bridal footwear, the coin is comfortably encased along the metal shank of the right shoe.

While Grace Kelly's bridal shoes were being created in New York, the prayer book she would carry on her wedding day was also being readied. Devout mid-twentieth-century brides often elected to carry a prayer book or Bible in place of a large bridal bouquet. Miss Kelly's specialized missal was a gift from

Above: An X ray of the wedding shoes reveals construction details and the lucky token. The side view of her left shoe shows the flat metal shank that supports the arch, the screw holding the shank in place, a round shank inside the heel, and the tacks attaching the sole to the upper. These tacks were driven against a metal last so the points turned over and clinched in place. Visible in the top view of her right shoe are the seed pearl and bead rosette on the vamp, the tacks at the heel, and the metal shank. Clearly outlined against the shank of her right shoe is the copper penny built into the shoe.

Right: David Evins and Grace Kelly examine her wedding shoes, but they are concealed from all but the bride-to-be by the cover of the handmade, lace-covered satin shoebox embroidered with the Monégasque royal shield. David Evins, master of high-fashion footwear in postwar America, sold shoes through exclusive shops and boutiques but also created made-to-order footwear for famous and wealthy clients; Miss Kelly was one of many who wore Evins shoes in both her professional roles and personal life. This visit in late March came at the height of her hectic New York wedding preparations, but the future bride looks undaunted in her jaunty sailor hat and managed to select numerous pairs of Evins shoes for her trousseau.

During the religious ceremony, Princess Grace carried this gilt-edged book, which contains a small crucifix inside the front cover. It is filled with prayers, hymns, meditations, and other information related to recent pontifical decrees. The book is covered with silk faille neatly affixed under the decorated endpapers and appliquéd with the same rose point lace used for the bride's dress. A border is formed by one of the lace motifs—stylized leaves made with alternating open and dense lace stitches—while roses with relief petals grace the corners. Seed pearls accent the lace and form a cross on the front.

Below: One of MGM's skilled embroiderers, whose name is unknown, puts the finishing touches on the book. Her hands show her age, which speaks to her years of experience.

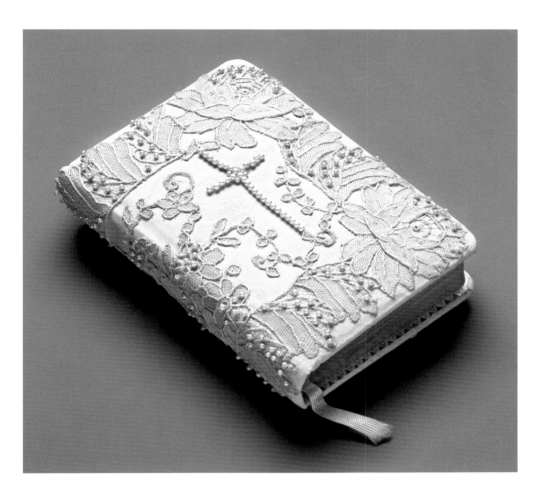

long-time friend of the Kelly family Mrs. John F. McClosky of Chestnut Hill. The book was sent to MGM to be decorated to match the wedding dress.

Once the MGM wardrobe department had completed the wedding gown, headpiece, veil, prayer book, and civil ceremony dress, the next challenge was how to get the delicate and voluminous garments safely to Monaco. In her book *Just Make Them Beautiful*, Helen Rose explained that the MGM prop department, accustomed to creating containers to send costumes on location, was consulted about the packing difficulties. Their solution was to create a huge aluminum box measuring about 7 by 4 feet. The gown, accessories, and civil ceremony dress, along with a white silk chiffon negligee ensemble from Miss Rose, were packed carefully into the box, with the wedding gown—"stuffed with hundreds of foam rubber pads and reams of tissue paper"—on top. According to Helen Rose: "It lay in the box like a beautiful stuffed doll. In among the tissue paper we placed pads of satin filled with cotton saturated with the most expensive French perfume we could find. When the box was opened after its long sea voyage, we wanted the dress not only to look like a picture but we wanted the aroma to be that of a thousand delicate flowers."

With so much interest and so much invested in the wedding gown, the studio decided not to let the precious box go on its journey to Monaco unaccompanied. Morgan Hudgins was sent to safeguard the dress as well as help the famous bride with press relations. Hudgins took his responsibility very seriously, riding on the truck to the airport and supervising the loading of the box into the plane's baggage compartment. The giant box made such a good story that several variations of its travels have been given. Miss Rose says it spent the night in New York with Hudgins at the Plaza Hotel, attracting suspicious stares when it was carried in, and then it occupied most of the space in his stateroom during the journey. Gant Gaither, who was on the voyage, recalled that Hudgins delivered the box to Miss Kelly's New York apartment, although the doorman initially tried to direct him to a nearby funeral home; it was then stowed in the ship's hold, where the bride's father checked on it during the voyage and found it turned on its end. In any event, Miss Rose reported that the wedding gown arrived in such perfect condition that it did not have to be ironed, although detailed pressing instructions in both French and English had been enclosed in case of this eventuality.

Joseph Hong displays his sketch for the attendants' dresses. Designers and manufacturers had clamored to get the prestigious assignment of creating "the most talked-about wedding party attire of this decade." Hong, who had briefly worked as a television staff artist, was not primarily interested in clothes—his previous design experience included everything from toys to greeting cards and stage sets. His sketch for the attendants' dresses was selected after Hong had worked in Neiman-Marcus's design department for only a few months. He saw the royal wedding as a modern-day fairy tale, and envisioned simple yet romantic dresses "that would fit the fairy-tale qualifications with a modern twist."

The Attendants' Dresses

On February 21, Grace Kelly announced the names of her bridal attendants. Her older sister, Margaret Davis, would be the matron of honor (her younger sister, Lizanne Levine, was expecting a baby in May and therefore unable to travel to Monaco). The other bridesmaids Miss Kelly selected were former schoolmates, professional friends, and roommates: Maree Frisby Pamp, Elizabeth (Bettina) Thompson Gray, Sally Parrish Richardson, Rita Gam, Carolyn Scott Reybold, and Judith Balaban Kanter. Prince Rainier's sister, Princess Antoinette, would also attend the bride.

The flower girls would be Margaret's daughters Margaret Ann (Meg), age nine, and Mary Lee, age seven, and Princess Antoinette's daughters Elisabeth, age nine, and Christine, age four. Princess Antoinette's son Christian, age seven, and the prince's distant cousin Sebastian von Furstenberg, age six, were selected as ring bearers.

As with the bride's dress, many in the fashion industry were very interested in designing and making the dresses for Miss Kelly's attendants. Among the most persistent was Neiman-Marcus, the department store headquartered in Dallas, Texas, from which the actress had received an award the previous fall. When Grace Kelly became engaged, president Stanley Marcus immediately asked if his store could provide the bridal gown and bridesmaid dresses. Because MGM was already giving the bride her dress, Neiman-Marcus was asked to submit a design for the attendants' dresses. The store apparently took the design challenge seriously, sending vice president Lawrence Marcus to Monaco to absorb the atmosphere and look at the cathedral. Neiman-Marcus submitted numerous sketches of possible bridesmaid dresses; Miss Kelly selected one of these, and Neiman-Marcus was given the commission. The store's involvement, announced at the same time as Miss Kelly's choice of bridal attendants, was, according to Stanley Marcus, "a great coup, which brought a tremendous amount of international press coverage, adding further prestige to our already famous bridal department."

The designer of the chosen sketch was Joseph Allen Hong, who was only twenty-five years old. Born in Texas to a Chinese American father and Mexican American mother, Hong grew up in California's Central Valley and attended the California College of Arts and Crafts in Oakland; in 1954, he joined the Army, and he had been stationed at Fort Bliss in Texas. Shortly after being discharged, he had been hired by Neiman-Marcus. Joseph Hong had initially been asked to help execute some preliminary sketches, but he threw in a few ideas of his own, and one of his designs was selected by the bride-to-be. The

Above: The identical dresses of the six bridesmaids and matron of honor all have labels to identify the wearer and the maker. Shown here are those from the dress worn by Margaret Kelly Davis (Gift of Mrs. John B. Kelly, 1963-52-1a). Inside the back waist is a standard "Neiman-Marcus Custom Made" label, machine stitched in metallic gold thread. Inside the back of the silk taffeta underbodice is a 4-by-6-inch silk satin label backstitched by hand with the name of the maker and the wearer in yellow silk embroidery floss.

Right: Bridesmaid's Dress and Petticoat. Designed by Joseph Hong (American, 1930–2004). Commissioned through Neiman-Marcus, Dallas (founded 1907). Made by Priscilla of Boston (founded 1950). 1956. Worn by Maree Rambo (then Maree Frisby Pamp). Dress: silk organdy over silk taffeta; petticoat: silk organdy over stiffened cotton. Gift of Mrs. Joseph S. Rambo, 1997-117-3a,b

A built-in strapless taffeta underdress is part of the organdy bridesmaid's dress. Beneath the small pointed collar are five decorative buttons, although the actual closure is at the side. The pleated sash is finished in back with three tailored bows. Both the skirt and underskirt are flat at the front waist, but the outer organdy layer is generously pleated around the back and sides, and the taffeta underskirt is heavily gathered in these areas. Synthetic horsehair sewn to the hems of both layers makes the skirts float beautifully, and a specially constructed silk organdy petticoat also supports the skirts. This petticoat has a fitted yoke above a full pleated skirt lined with stiff cotton fabric and is also banded with synthetic horsehair at knee level and at the hem.

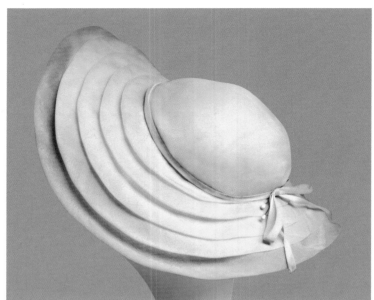

Above left: Bridesmaid's Hat. Designed by Joseph Hong (American, 1930–2004). Commissioned through Neiman-Marcus, Dallas (founded 1907). Made by Don Marshall (American, 1919–1995). 1956. Stitched synthetic horsehair, silk organza. Gift of Mrs. John B. Kelly, 1963-52-4

While the bridesmaids' dresses were marked with their names, the bridesmaids' hats were not; the only identification inside this hat is a "Neiman-Marcus Salon" label. The hat was painstakingly made by stitching very narrow synthetic horsehair in concentric circles; the rows of stitching are spaced only $1/8$ inch apart. The yellow horsehair forms a round crown and three overlapping brims, the edges of which are finished with a silk organza bias binding; a narrow silk organza bias tube also forms the tiny hatband and back bow. While the horsehair has a fair amount of body, a ring of yellow millinery wire was placed under the middle brim for added support to allow the outermost brim to undulate slightly around the bridesmaid's face. The hat was secured by two hair combs sewn inside the crown.

Above right: Matron of Honor's Hat. Designed by Joseph Hong (American, 1930–2004). Commissioned through Neiman-Marcus, Dallas (founded 1907). Made by Don Marshall (American, 1919–1995). 1956. Worn by Margaret Kelly Davis. Silk organza. Gift of Mrs. John B. Kelly, 1963-52-1b

Although the matron of honor's dress was identical to those of the bridesmaids, her hat was slightly different. It bears the same "Neiman-Marcus Salon" label as the others, but it is constructed of yellow organza and its brim is $1/2$ inch wider. The underbrim is formed by three concentric bias-cut organza circles, stiffened internally with millinery wire, while five narrower concentric circles make the top of the brim. The last of these circles extends out over the stiffened underbrim to give a very soft effect. The shallow, rounded crown is made of several layers of organza, and a narrow bias tube of the same fabric forms a band and a bow at back. To ensure the hat could be anchored at the proper angle, two combs were attached inside the crown and several hatpins, their tops covered in matching organza, were also provided.

young designer was quoted as saying that the commission to create the attendants' dresses was his "first big job of designing women's clothes."

The details of the attendants' dresses were confidential, and everyone involved was sworn to secrecy. In an interview on March 20, however, Joseph Hong gave a limited preview of the dresses, saying that cantaloupe was a "close guess" for the color and that he designed the covered-up, full-length gowns for what he called "a poignant, fantasy effect" in keeping with "the fairy-tale aspects of the romance between an American girl and a European monarch." The report from the International News Service also described the gowns as having "trend-setting back interest," a detail denied by Neiman-Marcus the following day. On March 25, Neiman-Marcus released descriptions and Hong's sketch of the dresses for the bridesmaids and flower girls. The bridesmaids' dresses and that of the matron of honor would all be identical; the design featured a high neckline with a small, pointed collar, tiny covered buttons down the front bodice, an obi-style sash with three folded bows in back, full bishop sleeves that extended below the elbow, and a fluid skirt of silk organdy over taffeta. Once the sketch was released, fashion reporters described the design as "high style," and especially commented on the long, wide skirt with what they called a "court train" that would "sweep the aisle with a foot or so of fabric"—this represented a departure from the ballet-length skirts favored for bridesmaids even for formal weddings in the months before the Monaco event. Miss Kelly's bridesmaids' dresses were said to be "marked by the same simplicity for which the bride-to-be is noted." The dresses were yellow—the bride's favorite color—in a shade called "Sunlight," which would provide a pleasing contrast to the grayness of Monaco's cathedral.

Once Neiman-Marcus had received the prestigious commission, they turned the construction of the bridesmaids' dresses over to the well-known bridal firm Priscilla of Boston. Priscilla Comins Kidder and her husband, James, anticipating an upswing in marriages after the Second World War, had opened a bridal boutique on Boston's Newbury Street in 1945; five years later the business became a wholesale producer of wedding gowns and bridal party dresses under the Priscilla of Boston label. By 1956, the firm had acquired fifteen hundred accounts from fashionable and important shops and department stores across the country, including Neiman-Marcus. When Mrs. Kidder got the important but "hush-hush" order at the beginning of March, some slight modifications were made in the design, perhaps at the bride's request. Hong had originally planned to use white for the dresses' wide sashes; in the final version the contrasting color scheme was eliminated, as were long streamers down the back. In the Priscilla of Boston factory on Newbury Street, the bridesmaids' dresses took shape in the hands of experienced seamstresses, many of them originally from Central Europe. Mrs. Kidder sadly told a reporter: "Custom sewing is disappearing as an art in this country. . . . Young girls don't seem to be interested in learning to sew. When the older women are gone, I don't know where we'll get people."

The Kidders drove the dresses to New York for two rounds of fittings, which took place at Miss Kelly's apartment on March 24 and March 28. During the fittings, Miss Kelly was in the next room choosing

Right: Flower Girl's Dress and Underdress. Designed by Joseph Hong (American, 1930–2004). Commissioned through Neiman-Marcus, Dallas (founded 1907). Made by Formals by Mary Carter, Dallas (founded 1952). 1956. Worn by Margaret Ann (Meg) Davis. Cotton organdy with silk machine embroidery, silk taffeta, lace. Gift of Mrs. John B. Kelly, 1963-52-2a,b

This dress was worn by Grace Kelly's oldest niece, Meg Davis, who celebrated her tenth birthday the day after she took part in the wedding in Monaco. Joseph Hong's design for the dress worn by the four flower girls echoed some of the features seen in his design for the adult attendants but also includes elements that were fashionable for girls' party dresses, such as very puffed sleeves and full short skirts. The sheer white organdy dress goes over a sheer yellow organdy underdress. This has a fitted bodice made from two layers of fabric, and its rounded neckline and armscyes are edged with narrow lace. The underdress has three very full skirts, including two of organdy (both edged with narrow lace); one of these skirts is made fuller by an additional deep ruffle at the hem. These skirts are attached to a yellow silk taffeta foundation skirt that is edged with synthetic horsehair inside the hem.

Above: Detail of Flower Girl's Dress. The sheer cotton organdy of the flower girl's dress is enlivened by sprigs of embroidered daisies. The daisy motifs alternate a stem of white daisies with yellow centers with yellow daisies with white centers. The motifs, nearly 3 inches tall, are spaced about 5 inches from each other in vertical rows. The machine embroidery is beautifully done to give each petal and leaf slight relief. The daisy theme of the flower girls was repeated in the halos of daisies that encircled their heads and the bouquets of tiny daisies they carried.

clothes for her trousseau. According to Mrs. Kidder, the bride was very easy to work with, liked the bridesmaids' dresses, and was "excited, enthusiastic, and interested in every detail." Under a tight schedule, the Kidders drove back to Boston through a terrible storm, did the final alterations, and brought the dresses back to New York on April 2, just in time for them to join the bridal party on the ship to Monaco. The execution of the dresses, said bridesmaid Bettina Gray, had involved "micrometric precision fittings," and consequently she had been ordered by Mrs. Kidder "not to gain a pound or put on a quarter of an inch" en route to Monaco because it would spoil the fit of the dress.

Joseph Hong's sketch of the attendants' dress included a shallow-crowned hat, inspired, the designer said, by the hats worn by ancient Greek shepherds. The hats' petal-like layers would be made of what was called misty hairbraid, and although they were intended to be accented with a small white butterfly bow at the back, the color contrast was eliminated when the white accents were removed from the dresses. Neiman-Marcus commissioned New York milliner Don Marshall to make the hats. Born in West Virginia as William Sydenstricker, the newly renamed Don Marshall appeared in Broadway choruses in the early

1940s; his millinery career began when he designed a hat for a fellow cast member. In 1945, he opened a millinery shop in New York, and by the mid-1950s, he had a salon in the East Fifties; the bridesmaids were given the telephone number of his shop and asked to call directly and set up their own fitting appointments. The yellow, tiered hats Marshall created used stitched synthetic horsehair for the bridesmaids and silk organdy for the matron of honor—both styles are masterpieces of millinery. According to bridesmaid Judith Kanter, the Kellys paid for the bridesmaids' dresses and hats, but each bought her own yellow-dyed, satin pumps and wrist-length, white kid gloves.

The design for the dress that the flower girls would wear was similar to that of the adult attendants, but Joseph Hong included features in keeping with the youthful age of the wearers. His sketch of the dress showed a pointed collar and a high pleated sash with back bows, short, puffed sleeves, and a full skirt that ended just below the knee. The dresses, worn over yellow organdy petticoats, were made of sheer white Swiss organdy embroidered with yellow and white sprigs of daisies. The design was executed by Formals by Mary Carter of Dallas, which designed and manufactured "youthful" formals and was founded in 1952 by Texas Women's University alumna Mary Carter. In the original sketch, the flower girl is shown in a hat matching that of the bridesmaid, but a simple wreath or halo of miniature daisies was substituted. The young attendants wore short white gloves, and their white Mary Janes and little white socks, recalled bridesmaid Judith Kanter, were purchased by mail order from the J. C. Penney catalogue by "thrifty Aunt Grace." The outfits of the two young ring bearers received little attention; they wore all white—the standard for ring bearers at the time—including full-sleeved shirts with ruffles down the front and at the wrists, satin knee breeches, stockings, and shoes with large buckles.

The Voyage to Monaco

At New York's Pier 84 on the morning of April 4, 1956, Grace Kelly boarded the S.S. *Constitution*, which, after an eight-day trip, would make a special stop to deliver the future bride. Miss Kelly did not set sail alone; the celebrated bride-to-be was "accompanied by an entourage of eighty and with sixty pieces of luggage and a trousseau befitting a princess."

Before the ship departed at noon, the bride held a press conference on the sun deck. Several hundred reporters, photographers, cameramen, and curiosity seekers caused a near riot with their pushing and shoving. The future princess, however, appeared "cool as a cucumber" as she fielded questions and bravely waved a white-gloved hand. Along with personal and general inquiries on various topics—her pet name for the prince, her future citizenship, her desired number of children, and the couple's plans for the honeymoon—the subject of clothes was raised. It was "the story feminine America has been breathless to hear: details of the trousseau of American-designed clothes." Miss Kelly responded to the question of how much luggage she had onboard by saying, "four trunks and quite a few suitcases and hatboxes." She had not brought her entire wardrobe with her—some of her trousseau purchases were not ready and would be brought by friends flying over for the wedding, and a trunk of favorite old clothes that included sneakers and jeans had already been shipped to Monaco.

Those accompanying Miss Kelly included her parents, other family members, some of the wedding party, friends, and a press party of almost two dozen (some of whom had to sleep in the ship's hospital). Miss Kelly spent the trip relaxing and enjoying the company of her family and friends, but the press was busy recording the hours she slept, the games of charades and shuffleboard she played, and, of course, the details of all her clothes. "All the passengers are waiting to see what Grace will wear," one newspaper reported, and those aboard were not alone—through photographs and reports, the press made sure the public knew all about Miss Kelly's onboard wardrobe, from a kelly green paper party hat donned at the first night's festivities to black slacks and a black sweater worn while dog walking. While her day clothes leaned toward casual skirts and practical headscarves, her evening attire included a dress from *High Society*, and she was seen in some of the new garments from her trousseau, many of which were beige or pastel. The press soon dubbed this the "Pale Princess" look.

The overseas trip was called a "floating fashion parade," and it was remarked, "Her Grace and the wedding party may have to change attire several times a day to wear all of the clothes they are taking on

Grace Kelly waving farewell to New York on April 4, 1956, aboard the S.S. Constitution, *surrounded by the press.* Women's Wear Daily *reported that, in addition to maintaining her ladylike demeanor, Miss Kelly "looked like a lady in her simple but chic and appropriate travel outfit, meticulously groomed as usual, and with an absence of clutter." She wears a lightweight spring wool suit—"inevitably beige"— with hip-length jacket and flared pleated skirt; the ready-to-wear ensemble by Ben Zuckerman was featured in* Harper's Bazaar's *March issue. Touches of white include her tambour hat with center self-bow from I. Magnin, chiffon scarf, and white eight-button fabric gloves. The exhaustive coverage of every detail of Miss Kelly's clothing even included the report that her stockings were seamless.*

the trip." Even the bride-to-be had joked, with a shake of her head, "I'm sure we're going to have to have another ship to accompany the *Constitution* so that we can carry all our luggage." In spite of the bride's extensive wardrobe—she reportedly wore a different evening dress every night—the press could not find enough to say to satisfy the fashion curious, so others in the wedding party became fodder for "news" stories. The bridesmaids' wardrobes were discussed and photographed, as were clothes of the mother of the bride; purchased in Philadelphia and Atlantic City, Mrs. Kelly's attire was said to be in "simple, classic lines with a youthful but dignified air." When all else failed, some newspapers wrote "long stories about the wardrobes of reporters and radio commentators bound for the wedding." On April 7, for example, the *Washington Post* published an article by Evelyn Hayes that was devoted to the sartorial challenges facing Hazel Markel, NBC's *Weekday Washington* reporter, detailing her choices for embarkation, the shipboard social schedule, and the upcoming events in Monaco. After this article appeared, one reporter remarked that this was "certainly the first time in the history of journalism that this has happened!"

In Monaco

On April 12, the S.S. *Constitution* arrived in Monaco; the small country had been "scrubbed like [a] new baby" and decorated top to toe. The ship dropped anchor a mile offshore, and a tender from the liner carried the future princess to meet her prince on his yacht, the *Deo Juvante II*. Their reunion took place on a gangplank between the two boats; Miss Kelly carried her poodle, Oliver, in her arms, which explained, at least to some, the lack of a kiss between the couple. Surrounded by press launches and speedboats, the yacht, under a shower of red and white carnations scattered from a plane above, brought the affianced pair and the bride's parents to shore. In the picturesque harbor, Miss Kelly disembarked and was greeted by an honor guard, officials, more flowers, and a stirring salute from horns and cannons. In addition, as many as fifty thousand spectators—twice the principality's population—gave her a warm ovation.

For her arrival in Monaco, Miss Kelly, who had reportedly been worried about what to wear, chose an extremely stylish ensemble recently purchased in New York. The sleeveless silk alpaca sheath topped by a matching coat was an off-the-rack Ben Zuckerman design in navy, the season's number one color. The coat featured a small collar, three-quarter-length sleeves, and a self-tie at the high waist above pleats.

Grace Kelly is welcomed to Monaco on April 12, 1956, as she steps ashore from her future husband's yacht in the harbor. Followed closely by the prince, the famous bride-to-be carries her poodle—complete with white leash and bow—and wears a stylish navy Ben Zuckerman coat and large white hat. In the background, the buildings of the rocky principality "stand on each other's heads" as they rise up the hillside. Along with many of Monaco's twenty thousand residents, her welcoming committee included thousands of other cheering spectators and more than a thousand reporters who had descended on Monaco to cover the wedding.

The waistline—a departure from the previous year's dropped waist—was very much *à la mode*: "The only females wearing long torsos this year will be those who didn't buy a new Easter outfit and those under ten." A bunch of imitation white violets adorned the front of the coat just as they did in Zuckerman's ad in *Harper's Bazaar* in February, but the bride-to-be personalized her outfit with pearl earrings and bracelet, a white scarf crossed inside her V neckline, and short white gloves. By this time, white gloves were not only a "Kelly trademark" but, in a direct contribution to fashion from Miss Kelly, "the glove to wear." It was the hat she chose, however, that received the most attention and a fair amount of criticism.

Made of white organdy, this chapeau had a huge mushroom-shaped brim that was "as big as a manhole cover." The size and shape were the height of current fashion, but the windy day meant that Miss Kelly had to hold on to "her flying saucer hat," which threatened to take wing and "fly her off the deck." In addition, the orchid lei with which she was presented did not fit over it and had to be taken apart. The main charge leveled against the hat, however, was that the broad, downturned brim hid Miss Kelly's famously beautiful face from her future subjects and eager photographers. A closed car soon whisked Miss Kelly off to the palace, where she made a brief appearance to wave from the balcony and then retired. The cartwheel hat—the creation of Countess Ann Valde of Philadelphia—continued to be discussed. The Associated Press, for example, picked up the remarks of Monsignor Joseph A. McCaffrey at a New York communion breakfast: "I have heard the creator of Miss Kelly's hat has said she will never make another hat like it. It is the hope of everyone who saw that hat that she will keep her vow."

Interest in the wedding was so intense that the coverage threatened to validate humorist Art Buchwald's prediction of "a simple wedding ceremony with only 450 invited guests and 340,986 members of the working press." As the event drew near, the hysteria mounted. Newspapers and other media outlets began to hype their coverage of the bridal extravaganza. On April 4, the *Boston Daily Globe* pledged, "There won't be a stone left unturned—or a diamond or ruby for that matter." Three top women reporters, the newspaper promised, will "tell the girls back home what they would look for if they were present in person," while "the man's viewpoint" would be covered by a male reporter "who usually keeps an eye on more significant European matters." In addition, the newspaper would have reports from their wire service, the Associated Press, the United Press, and Reuters, and images would come from an equally impressive group of photographers. On April 8, the *Post-Standard* of Syracuse, New York, touted its wedding coverage at the bottom of its front page: "Are you interested in the wedding of Grace Kelly and Prince Rainier? Who isn't? *The Post-Standard's* EXCLUSIVE coverage of this royal event will be THE GREATEST!" Outlining their "intimate dispatches" and other features, the paper entreated, "Consider this your invitation to the most glamorous wedding of the decade—via your *Post-Standard!*" Others took a more grandiose tack: an advertisement for *TV Guide* was in the form of an invitation to the wedding, complete with crown and crest, with "the honour of your presence" requested by "Special Television Coverage."

Numerous reporters and other staff members were sent to Monaco by the various competing news organizations. The United Press sent actress Gloria Swanson to Monaco to report on the wedding, and others mustered their top talent to try to have sufficient coverage to satisfy public interest and scoop the competition. To deal with the 1,000 reporters that were expected, a press center was opened in Monaco, and a beaming official, certain that nothing was forgotten, proclaimed, "I believe this is the first press center in the world to have both a religious chapel and a serpentine bar." But even the most thorough preparations were not enough. By April 16, the Monégasque press chief reported 1,800 had been accredited to cover the wedding—200 more than covered the 1955 summit in Geneva. Noting that the Associated Press contingent in Monaco included seven correspondents, five photographers, and innumerable technical assistants, columnist John Crosby declared he was left with "the distinct impression that news in the rest of the world will stop dead in its tracks from now until the honeymoon." Crosby saw this as confirmation that Americans "prefer fairy tales to the stark nonfiction of everyday life." While a few others also saw the nuptial monomania as evidence that society was losing a just sense of proportion, a "sad commentary on our own judgment," many shared the feelings of the writer of a letter printed in the *Boston Daily Globe*; the couple's sense of duty and dignity, the writer believed, was a fine example to modern youth and gave optimists reason to rejoice.

After the bride-to-be's safe arrival, the numerous and lavish wedding week celebrations could begin. Early in the wedding preparations, the prince was reported to have ordered, "I want the richest ceremonial of the past revived for my beautiful wife." He and his staff had painstakingly planned not only the two marriage ceremonies but also a full schedule of receptions, galas, dinners, ballets, athletic events, fireworks, and other celebratory fetes. One couple was reported to have calculated that to attend all the events to which they were invited in Monaco would have required twenty-three separate costumes for her as well as a new wardrobe for him; although reasonably wealthy, they couldn't afford this outlay and sent their regrets, much to the incredulity of those desperately seeking invitations. Indeed, it was generally agreed that any of the "starry-eyed stay-at-homes" would "give [their] eyeteeth to see Grace Kelly become the bride of a prince." Everyone wanted to participate, and almost thirty thousand visitors were expected during the wedding week. Some of those in Monaco not invited to the wedding were said to have ordered "an impressive array of glad-rags to be worn, apparently, while viewing the televised ceremony."

To those who were going to the wedding, the prospect of the wedding parties brought out "the clothes horse and the real jewels in women." European guests ordered their clothes from Parisian designers such as Jean Dessès and Balmain and Roman fashion houses such as Antonelli and Sorelle Fontana. American guests preferred U.S. designers such as Galanos, Pattullo-Jo Copeland, Nettie Rosenstein, and Traina-Norell. One commentator succinctly summarized the embarrassment of riches: "Never have so many women brought so much luggage to such a small country for so few days."

The finery brought by visitors proved to be very tempting—a friend of the Kelly family and one of the bridesmaids had jewels worth many thousands of dollars stolen from their hotel rooms (events reported with fervor by the press). Not all the clothes worn in Monaco were elaborate; a minor clothing-related sensation was caused when Grace Kelly's sister and nieces were seen strolling in Bermuda shorts, an informality that caused "some lifted eyebrows."

While men's clothing for wedding-related parties attracted much less attention, it did not go unnoticed. Although men had only a few options—full dress of white tie and tails, a dinner suit or tuxedo,

During the week before the wedding, numerous celebratory events kept the bride and groom, wedding guests, and journalists busy. On April 16, more than fifty photographers were allowed to record the rehearsal for the cathedral wedding. In this photograph, the ring bearers and flower girls, flanked by the matrons of honor, are directed by the Monégasque chamberlain and the bride, who wears a trim suit, gloves, turban, and sunglasses. Grace Kelly's father thought it was bad luck for the bride to practice her bridal walk, so her mother stood in for her.

formal morning dress of a cutaway with striped trousers, or a business suit—choosing the correct apparel could be confusing. Hotelier Conrad Hilton, President Eisenhower's personal representative to the wedding, revealed that the State Department had sent him a short note outlining "what pants to wear on which occasions."

The wedding week was extraordinarily busy, and the press was increasingly demanding. The volume of reporters dispatched to Monaco for the so-called W-Day overwhelmed the tiny country; many of them referred to its approximately 370 acres by disparaging names such as "pinpoint municipality," "postage stamp realm," "midget monarchy," "pint-size" or "pre-shrunk principality," and "rococo little country." With so many reporters searching such a small place for unique angles, the level of coverage was intense. News organizations rushed to get the latest scoop; when no information was forthcoming, they invented new angles to cover. One continuing speculation centered on whether the prince would dance with his slightly taller bride. The Hearst syndicate had contracted for the exclusive rights to publish a new song called *The Prince and Princess Waltz*. There was thus great relief when their reporter Dorothy Kilgallen could trumpet the news that the couple was indeed observed publicly dancing cheek-to-cheek.

After her arrival, Miss Kelly enjoyed a few days of seclusion and attended to such details as the final fittings for her wedding dress. She and the prince drove to a family luncheon at his sister's villa only to have their car mobbed by photographers; the prince reacted by barring the press from some upcoming events. The first big function, a dinner-dance at the casino, was given by Mr. and Mrs. Kelly on April 14. The next night, the couple attended a white-tie gala at the International Sporting Club that aimed to re-create the splendor of Versailles; Miss Kelly—the most simply dressed woman there—wore a pale blue gown and was "a picture of fragile loveliness," but when she and the prince failed to stop for photographs as they left in the rain, they were booed by the soggy and disappointed press. With the help of publicist Morgan Hudgins, cordial relations were restored, and at the rehearsal of the wedding in the cathedral of Saint Nicolas on the morning of April 16, more than fifty photographers were allowed to record the event. The prince was more jovial, and the bride, efficient in a beige suit, white turban, and white gloves, removed her glasses when asked. By the end of the pre-wedding celebrations, however, it was reported that, while thrilled and overwhelmed by the exciting events of the preceding week, Miss Kelly had repeatedly sighed, "I'll be glad to get on that yacht." Prince Rainier, also looking forward to a peaceful honeymoon, had commented, "All I want to do is get as far out to sea as I can."

The Wedding Dress Revealed

On April 17, a day before the civil ceremony, details of Miss Kelly's wedding gown were released by MGM. The information, according to *New York Times* special reporter Henry Giniger, was "considered the biggest news thus far communicated to the press." The long-awaited details of the dress were printed around the country, as were Helen Rose's sketches showing the front and back of the formal gown for the religious ceremony and her drawing of the lace suit for the civil ceremony. Once again, reporters sought superlatives: The United Press declared, "MGM made sure the bride's costume would be the most supercolossal ever worn by a film star," while the International News Service described the cathedral dress as "the most lavish ever worn by a bride."

According to reports, the studio announcement "raved the dress was so expensive 'the cost would be prohibitive if made by a private coutourier [*sic*].'" Helen Rose was quoted as saying she couldn't possibly estimate the cost "because we used all studio help," and she further confided, "It frightens me to think of it." She later called the dress the most expensive wedding gown she had ever designed. Other experts were consulted; Hollywood designer Marusia, who had made a number of wedding gowns for movie stars, said the most expensive ran about $1,800. "But I imagine Miss Kelly's must have cost at least $2,500 or $3,000." Historian Stephen Englund, who had access to the MGM archives, states in his biography of Princess Grace that the cost of the dress was in fact $7,266.68 in materials and manufacture, not including Helen Rose's salary. Regardless of this often-repeated figure's accuracy, the dress was certainly expensive. Mal Caplan, head of MGM's wardrobe department, later recalled that its high cost had caused some concern at MGM: "When the estimate went to the studio heads for approval, they balked because of the cost. But Howard Strickling [head of publicity] had it approved, saying that the very privilege of presenting the gown to the Princess of Monaco completely justified any cost."

If the cost of the dress was great, the other numbers given out by the studio were equally grand. According to the news release, the "full recipe" for the gown included "25 yards of heavy taffeta (*peau de soie*), 25 yards of silk taffeta, 100 yards of silk net, and 300 yards of lace." When this information was printed throughout the country, a few newspapers did note that the reported 300 yards of lace were narrow strips of Valenciennes, or Val, lace; most, however, preferred merely to repeat the large numbers, and some even added them up to get headlines such as "400 Yards in Gown for Grace," or made statements that the bride's costume "used up 450 yards of material." These exaggerated estimates, repeated over and over, have left the lasting impression of the beautiful bride surrounded by a sea of fabric. MGM may have indeed purchased such vast quantities, but the finished dress, full-skirted and petticoated though it was, did not actually use even a quarter of the amounts given. Common sense, however, was not applied in most reports about the "fairy-tale" gown.

*After months of tight security and intense mystery, Helen
Rose's design for Grace Kelly's wedding dress was revealed
two days before the religious wedding ceremony. This sketch
was signed by the designer, who most likely created this
important drawing herself. Because she sometimes designed
for up to seven films simultaneously, Miss Rose customarily
made only a rough sketch of a costume design, and her
assistant rendered the final color drawing for use by the
producer, director, star, and wardrobe department. MGM
noted with pride that it took thirty-five milliners, beaders,
seamstresses, embroiderers, and dyers nearly two months
to make this "supercolossal" gown.*

While the quantities of the fabric and lace were confusing, so were the historically complex terms
used to describe the materials. The lace used for the bodice and on the veil, train insert, and prayer
book was called rose point lace, a name given when this lace was introduced in the mid-nineteenth century because of its elaborate floral decoration. Several other names can also be applied to rose point
lace. Because it is made with a threaded needle using variations of the buttonhole stitch, the most basic
classification for rose point lace is needle lace or needlepoint lace. Rose point lace can also be called
Brussels lace or Brussels point since it was made in and around Brussels from the mid-nineteenth to the
early twentieth century. Finally, the term *point de gaze* is used for the lace (especially in Europe)
because one of its distinguishing characteristics is a delicate, filmy gauze mesh ground made of simple
buttonhole stitches worked in rows.

Rose point lace was one of the most delicate and expensive laces of the mid- to late nineteenth century and was extremely popular for dresses, shawls, flounces, parasols, handkerchiefs, and fans, and also
used for bridal veils. The decorative motifs in rose point lace can include roses and other flowers with
offshoots, branches, leaves, and tendrils, which may be complemented by swags and scrolls and dotted
throughout with sprigs, small blossoms, or tiny rings of tight buttonhole stitches. As rose point lace techniques advanced in the second half of the nineteenth century, extra petals were partially attached to the
rose motifs to give them additional relief. Although the lace making industry had declined by the mid-
twentieth century, rose point lace remained popular for bridal wear, especially veils. In her 1953 book,
Lace and Lace-Making, Marian Powys begins the chapter on bridal laces by stating, "Rose point is the
best-loved lace in America and it always has great glamour and charm."

The ruffles that cover the built-in skirt support and ruffled petticoat that hold up the full skirt of
Grace Kelly's wedding dress (see Appendix, page 72) are of Valenciennes lace. A type of bobbin lace
made by interlacing threads taken from specialized bobbins (elongated spools) for ease of handling,
authentic Valenciennes lace requires great skill to make since both the pattern and ground are made in
one step using continuous threads. While it took its name from the town on the French-Belgian border
where it was first made, Valenciennes became very popular in the mid-seventeenth century and was soon
made in other areas. In the late nineteenth century, Valenciennes was often made in Belgium, although
the continuous thread technique was no longer used. By this time, Valenciennes lace could also be
successfully imitated by machine, as the lace on the wedding underpinnings shows.

Even the relatively straightforward skirt fabric could be called by several names. The skirt is made of
a plain-weave silk fabric that can simply be called taffeta; it has a fine horizontal rib, which means it
can also generically be called faille. However, other more esoteric terms were also used. The studio
called the fabric *peau de soie*, a late-nineteenth-century term that in the mid-1950s described a firm,
soft silk with a dull, satinlike finish. Another late-nineteenth-century term, *gros de Londres*, was also

Left: Detail of the rose point lace on the train insert

*The wedding dress uses motifs from a length of rose point
lace made of fine cotton thread. The motifs were cut away
from the original mesh ground, or réseau, and artfully
rearranged. As this detail shows, the motifs are enhanced by
a raised outline, or cordonnet, that is made by placing a
group of threads around the edge of a motif and affixing it
with buttonhole stitches. Intricate decorative stitches within
rose point motifs produce a variety of textures, and the inter-
play between densely packed and widely spaced stitches
gives the effect of shading. The wedding dress lace was then
delicately accented with seed pearls.*

*Right: Detail of the Valenciennes lace on a ruffle of the
skirt support*

*During the late nineteenth and early twentieth centuries,
edgings and insertions of machine-made Valenciennes lace
were very popular as trimming on clothing and undergarments.
Valenciennes edgings are characterized by mesh grounds
and by a scalloped edge decorated with picots (tiny loops).
The machine-made cotton Valenciennes lace edging used on
Grace Kelly's petticoats features a pattern of small flowers
and diamonds of dots that is typical of this lace; such simple
designs remain effective when gathered, as they are on her
built-in petticoats.*

Designed by
Helen Rose

Opposite: Back view of Princess Grace's Wedding Dress

Helen Rose's design for the wedding dress reflects her belief that, since a bride faces the altar, the back of the gown should be a focal point. Although the circular veil is waist-length in front, it lengthens in back to flow over the full skirt, where its sheerness allows the large silk faille bows to be seen. Two tiny appliquéd lace lovebirds were placed at the back of the veil above the lace edging. Where the lace on the back of the veil ends, the lace of the train begins, and the skirt opens to reveal a triangular insert of floral lace motifs on tulle (see Appendix, page 72). The scalloped edge of the insert fans out elegantly to form the center of the train, while the back and sides of the skirt are deeply pleated to allow the silk faille to flow gracefully behind the bride.

Right: Princess Grace's Wedding Headpiece. Designed by Helen Rose (American, 1904–1985). Made by the wardrobe department of MGM, Culver City, California (founded 1924). 1956. Rose point lace, seed pearls, wax and paper orange blossoms, wire frame. Gift of Her Serene Highness, the Princesse Grace de Monaco, 1956-51-4a

The wedding cap, designed to match the bridal dress perfectly, is made from the same rose point lace and embellished with lustrous seed pearls. A wire framework supports the delicate lace, which, like the lace of the dress bodice, has been reassembled to complement the shape of the piece. The back of the cap (top right) has a central lace rose motif adorned with raised petals and pearl-loop stamens; it is surrounded by an edging of the lace leaf motif that also finishes the bodice neck and sleeves. The shape of the wire foundation creates a crownlike effect, which is enhanced by a wreath of orange blossoms, seed-pearl leaves, and tiny wired lace motifs.

The detail of the headpiece at bottom right shows the richness of the pearl-encrusted lace and the components of the floral wreath. The central peak of the cap comes nearly to the hairline; the added semi-circle of relief petals with three pearl-loop stamens is clearly visible. Each of the peaks at the sides of the cap also has a central lace rose. The wreath is given depth by three elements: delicate wax orange blossoms with tiny paper stamens; openwork leaves of seed pearls; and small floral lace motifs that have been stiffened, wired, and dotted with seed pearls. All three are affixed to wire stems that cause them to stand gracefully around the cap.

used to refer to the fine silk faille; to add to the confusion, *gros de Londres* could be sometimes miscon-strued as "gros de longre" (the term Helen Rose uses in her book *Just Make Them Beautiful*).

According to the studio announcement, the wedding gown was "in regal style designed along Renaissance lines." The long-sleeved bodice was constructed by placing rose point lace over thin silk gauze; the lace, in a wheat and flower pattern, had been re-embroidered so no seams were visible. The "bell-shaped" silk faille skirt was without folds in front, but it was heavily pleated in back; the three petticoats and the 14-inch-long skirt support that held out the dress were described as a "masterpiece of engineering." The headpiece was called a Juliet cap (while defined as a small, round, jeweled cap, this term was often used for any type of small headpiece) made of rose point lace and decorated with a wreath of delicate wax orange blossoms imported from France and leaves fashioned from tiny pearls. The circular veil, intended to keep the bride's face on view, was also embellished with rose point lace motifs, including two tiny lovebirds, and accented with seed pearls.

In publicizing the details of their magnificent creation, MGM naturally tended toward hyperbole, generating inaccurate information that has been repeated ever since. They stated, for example, that the gown's strapless underbodice and petticoats could be worn separately as an evening dress, which is patently impossible given that these were built into the bodice and skirt. They also said the fan-shaped train was 3 1/2 yards long, but it actually trails on the ground for about 3 feet, forming a graceful but not excessive train. In the same vein, the lace was repeatedly described as 125 years old, which means it would have been made around 1830. While undoubtedly a fine piece of old lace, the techniques used to create it date from the late nineteenth century. Doubt must also be cast on the oft-repeated story, perhaps started by Helen Rose, that the rose point lace had been purchased from a French museum for $2,500. The valuable lace was probably purchased from a dealer, since museums are not in the habit of selling their objects.

MGM also provided a description of the outfit Grace Kelly would wear for the civil ceremony. This ensemble, while "naturally not so elaborate as the formal gown," was "designed with equal care." Miss Kelly would wear a lace suit described as "hand-run Alençon lace of blush tan fitted over ashes of roses taffeta." (The fashion-speak of the announcement was confusing even at the time—at least one paper mistranslated "blush"—a very pale beige—as "bluish," but correctly deciphered "ashes of roses" as "dusty rose.") The announcement and sketch revealed a snugly fitting suit jacket with a high neckline, small collar, and silk-cord bow above a row of lace-covered buttons down the front. A matching full, flared skirt was hemmed to 14 inches from the floor. A small, close-fitting cloche hat, trimmed with silk flowers, matched the lace suit; pumps by David Evins and short white gloves completed the civil ceremony ensemble.

The Civil Wedding

On the morning of April 18, Grace Kelly and Prince Rainier were wed in a forty-minute civil ceremony as required by the civil code of Monaco. The wedding was held in the throne room of the palace in front of approximately eighty guests—a number that included representatives from twenty-four nations. The bride, beautiful in her lace suit, appeared strained, serious, and, by some reports, tearful; the groom, wearing formal morning dress, seemed nervous and fidgety, and he continuously ran his finger inside his collar. The solemn ceremony was performed by Marcel Portanier, Monaco's minister of justice and the highest legal authority in the principality. After the two had agreed to take each other as husband and wife, they were pronounced united in the bonds of marriage in the eyes of the law. The prince and his bride, now Her Serene Highness Grace Patricia of Monaco, signed the marriage registry, the bride removing one short white glove to do so. They exchanged a shy glance but no kiss and reenacted part of the ceremony for film cameras.

Now legally wed, the couple celebrated at a garden party for 2,500 Monégasque subjects. In the palace garden, the prince and new princess seemed to relax, drinking champagne and smiling radiantly. That night they attended the opera gala, the most elaborate wedding-related festivity; in one reporter's superlatives, it promised to be "the biggest thing since Ben Hur or the winning of the West." Female guests were resplendent in jewels and ball gowns, although according to bridesmaid Bettina Gray, the bride had warned some of the female guests that their formal long gowns for this event should not have too many petticoats because the seats were small. One American wistfully commented, "The clothes are magnificent, but I wish they had tags so you could tell if they were Diors or Lanvins or Balmains." In a nod to Parisian designers and to her future father-in-law's family, who owned the French couture house, Miss Kelly had ordered a dress for this event from Lanvin in early March; in Monaco, a special envoy from the couture house had ensured a perfect fit. The glittering high-waisted dress, made of ivory silk organdy embroidered with thousands of sequins, pearls, and rhinestones, was designed by Antonio Castillo in what was dubbed "the Goya manner." It had, however, been specially created as a background for the princess's decorations and orders, which included the red and white ribbon of the Monégasque Order of Saint Charles that the prince had just given her. Thus clad, and wearing a diamond tiara and necklace that she had been given by the people of Monaco, the new Princess Grace looked entirely regal.

Prince Rainier and the new Princess Grace of Monaco, now legally married, celebrate after the civil ceremony on April 18, 1956. The bridal dress for the legal rites, like the one for the religious ceremony, was designed by Helen Rose and created by the MGM wardrobe department. The dress, more properly described as a lace suit, consisted of a fitted bodice with high rounded collar and a flared skirt. MGM workers re-embroidered the outlines of the floral-patterned lace in dusty pink silk floss to give the fabric what Miss Rose described as a very unusual effect. The civil wedding ensemble was harmoniously completed by a cloche hat, short gloves, and David Evins–designed shoes.

The Cathedral Wedding

On the morning of April 19, the sun finally shone for what was billed as the "wedding of the century." On the cathedral steps, a red carpet and white silk wedding canopy enlivened the scene, as did a cordon of honor including firemen and carabineers as well as American sailors and boy scouts. More than five hundred wedding guests formed "a glittering assemblage of lesser European royalty, millionaires, diplomats, friends, and families of the couple." Ava Gardner, Somerset Maugham, former King Farouk of Egypt, and the Aga Khan and his wife were among the notables. Guests were asked to arrive at the cathedral no later than nine thirty, but many were slow to take their seats as they watched other guests arrive.

Some guests had fretted about what to wear. Sticklers for etiquette knew that correct daytime formal wear for men was a gray cutaway coat and striped trousers. "Brand new protocol" for the wedding, however, decreed that male guests wear full uniform with decorations or white tie and tails; the fathers of both the bride and groom and Monégasque officials wore continental tails of midnight blue—a popular midcentury choice said to look blacker than black at night—over matching trousers with braided stripes. Top hats were also worn.

Although they had been asked to wear short, covered-up neutral dresses, women came dressed in everything from simple suits to evening gowns. The cold and gloomy weather earlier that week had led to reports that some wedding guests had purchased warm woolen underwear to wear under their summery wedding finery. Many wore mink stoles or capes, hats were of every size and shape, and coat or jacket and dress ensembles were popular. Full-skirted monotone outfits in beige or pastel hues predominated, but Mrs. Cornelius Vanderbilt Whitney "caught every eye as she arrived clad in shocking pink from her huge hat to shoes." Once again, women "were divided as to [the nationalities of] their dressmakers in accordance with their home address."

At eight that morning, the bridesmaids and the two Philadelphia flower girls were picked up from their hotel by limousines. At the palace, the bridesmaids fluffed the full sleeves of their Joseph Hong organdy dresses, and, as their petticoat-supported skirts flowed gracefully around them, adjusted their hats to get the correct angle; each carried a nosegay of yellow rosebuds.

Because of the complexity of her dress, the bride had practiced getting into it several times, and Helen Rose had also sent instructions for how to put the four parts on, which Virginia Darcy had helped decode. That morning, the bride donned the complicated creation for her wedding day.

The first part of the dress put on was the lace bodice with attached underbodice, slip, and skirt support (see Appendix, page 72). The front of the silk underbodice was zipped up and hooked together; then the two dozen tiny lace-covered buttons of the lace bodice were fastened through corresponding loops, and the dozen buttons at each wrist were also done up. The silk satin slip with a deep lace border extended from the waist, as did the skirt support that was held out by a hoop and covered with lace-edged ruffles. The outer skirt of fine silk faille, heavily pleated at the waist, was put on over the slip and skirt support. Attached to the inside of the skirt were tiers of stiff lace-edged net ruffles that were dotted at intervals with little blue satin bows; smoothed by a silk taffeta overlayer, the ruffles also gave the outer skirt the planned shape. At the back, the skirt fanned out gracefully into the 3-foot train. At the back of the skirt's waistband, a triangular panel—lace on silk net over taffeta and stiff net—was snapped into place. Three large silk bows were snapped closed down the center back across the lace insert, which cascaded out into the train. The pleated silk faille cummerbund was then put around the bride's waist (smaller than ever since she had lost weight under the strain of wedding preparations) and fastened by silk-faille-covered buttons at the back.

With the dress on, the headpiece of lace was fit onto the bride's sleekly pulled-back hair. The millinery-wire foundation formed three peaks in front, the center one extending nearly to her hairline. Around the raised crown in back, an elegant wreath was formed by traditional bridal orange blossoms complemented by tiny leaves made of seed pearls and small, wired floral lace motifs. The large, circular veil, embellished around the edge with lace motifs and tiny seed pearls, had been slightly gathered into the back of the cap to fall gracefully over her large chignon. Only the sheerest silk tulle covered her face, which was set off by discreet pearl earrings. The front edge of the veil came to her waist, but the back flowed down to meet the lace of the train insert. Peeping from beneath the hem of the dress were the matching lace wedding slippers.

The lace bodice, skillfully re-embroidered by two skilled seamstresses who worked on it for a month, fit perfectly. The delicate lace came up the sides of the princess's neck, where the edges were seamlessly finished in scalloped-edged motifs. The long lace sleeves extended over the back of her hands, where they also terminated gracefully in small scallops. On each side of the bodice front, lace scrolls and floral motifs were expertly placed to balance the design, and the back of the bodice featured radiating flower stems as its focal point. Thousands of tiny seed pearls accented the pattern of the lace. On both the bodice and the cap, selected floral motifs were given depth by the addition of semicircles of raised petals; from under these petals, loops of seed pearls formed elegant stamens. On the bodice front, these pearl loops hung down and could move slightly, as could those on the cap, where a slightly longer single string of seed pearls gave even greater movement. Only the pearl loops that pointed up on the bodice back had been tacked in place to prevent drooping. The gown's full skirt was flat at the front but deeply pleated at the back and sides, which made it spring out gracefully from the waist. The cummerbund, which further set off the waist, rose in gentle folds to just under the bust. Helen Rose's design, from the soft ivory color of the lace, silk, and pearls to the overall simplicity of the gown, enhanced the bride's ethereal, elegant beauty.

Although Grace Kelly had played brides in High Noon and High Society, those roles had not called for traditional bridal gowns; thus, her appearance in the wedding dress that had been so secretly and laboriously made was much anticipated. Indeed, the dress was considered of such significance that one press report referred to Helen Rose's creation as Grace Kelly's "co-star" at the ceremony. The dress's soft ivory color, flowing lines, and romantic simplicity perfectly suited the elegant royal bride. A spectator in the crowd was reported to have exclaimed, "She's too beautiful to be real."

The bride held her small lace-and-pearl encrusted prayer book and a loose arrangement of lilies of the valley, which was finished with hanging silk ribbons that had flowers decorating their ends. For "something borrowed," she also carried a handkerchief, one which she had lent to her sister Lizanne to use at her wedding and which her sister had lent back to her for this occasion.

Once dressed, the bride greeted her attendants, and they all posed for photographs inside the palace in the white-and-gold salon and then outside in the Galerie d'Hercule. The group then went down the curving stairs into the palace courtyard, and the attendants walked the hundred yards to the cathedral, arriving at ten-thirty as planned. The bride, accompanied by her father, got into a black Rolls-Royce, delicately lifting her skirts as palace staff held her train and veil aloft. Inside the cathedral, guests had been seated, white flowers were everywhere, and television and newsreel cameras and microphones hung from the rafters. The groom's mother and father, their aides, the bride's mother, and other family members had just taken their places.

In a departure from American matrimonial traditions, the bride and her father entered the cathedral first and walked down the aisle. Princess Grace took her place at the *prie-dieu*, with her family's parish priest at her side. The two ring bearers, holding white satin cushions, entered, followed by the four flower girls, carrying their daisy bouquets. The matron of honor went down the aisle, and then the bridesmaids followed in pairs. The attendants went to their pews on the right of the aisle. The bride's sister took her place as matron of honor nearest the altar; the groom's sister also served as a matron of honor, but she did not walk in the procession and wore a white-and-gold brocade full-length floating coat by Castillo for Lanvin rather than a bridesmaid's dress.

The royal groom followed a few moments later, wearing a wedding outfit he had designed himself. Based on the uniform of Napoleon's marshals, his black tunic was decorated with gold embroidered cuffs and epaulettes, and his sky blue trousers had a thick gold stripe down the sides. The prince's chest was embellished with medals and orders, the red and white sash of the Order of Saint Charles extended diagonally from shoulder to waist, and gold cords looped across it on the right; his sword hung from a red and gold belt. As he entered the cathedral, Prince Rainier, accompanied by his witnesses, carried a midnight blue bicorne with white ostrich feathers. He was met at the altar by his personal chaplain, the chamberlain, and the bishop of Monaco—all resplendent in the brilliant clothing of their positions.

The ceremony was conducted solemnly, with organs, a choir, and an orchestra adding music to the occasion. The bishop of Monaco gave a short speech and then asked the prince and the princess if they took each other in marriage according to the rite of the church. After both said *oui* and rings had been exchanged, the bride's parish priest spoke, and the bishop celebrated a communion mass. A papal emissary offered the pope's blessing and delivered an address. Then the prince and princess proceeded slowly down the aisle, with what the *New Yorker* later called "Miss Kelly's ascension to serenity" complete. Outside the cathedral, as trumpets sounded, they took their places in an open-top cream and black Rolls-Royce, a gift from the Monégasque people. With the rest of the bridal party following in limousines, the royal couple's motorcade drove slowly through the streets of Monaco as thousands waved

Opposite: Princess Grace praying during the solemn nuptial mass. In this view the details of the cap and gown can be appreciated; the seed-pearl strand that dangles from the side of her cap is echoed by the bride's pearl earring. The scalloped edges of the lace bodice at the neck and wrists feature alternating areas of open and dense lace stitches. The lace forms a carefully arranged, intricate pattern of swirls, leaves, and flowers over the rest of the bodice; its texture and three-dimensional elements are visible on the princess's elbows and forearms. From beneath the cummerbund, the deep, closely spaced pleats at the back of the skirt spring out gracefully.

Below: Inside the cathedral, the groom has joined the bride at the altar. The bride's sister stands beside her as matron of honor, while the bridesmaids and flower girls are in their places on the other side of the aisle. Surrounded by officials in court uniforms, altar boys in white robes, and members of the clergy in richly embroidered vestments, Prince Rainier and Princess Grace are united in marriage by the bishop of Monaco. Also surrounding the couple were innumerable cameras and microphones to broadcast the ceremony to a fascinated world.

joyfully and church bells pealed. The procession stopped at the tiny church of Sainte Dévote, named after the patron saint of Monaco, and here, too, the scene was enlivened by brilliant clothing, for the route was lined with hundreds of Monégasque schoolgirls wearing red and white dresses that had been given to them by the prince. The bride left her bouquet as an offering to the saint, a Monégasque wedding tradition, and the couple returned to the palace.

The newlyweds, after posing for more photographs, appeared at the palace window to greet the thousands of people waiting outside, and then they descended the stairs to join their guests in the courtyard of the palace. The couple cut the five-tiered wedding cake with the groom's sword, and an elegant buffet luncheon was served. After some time spent greeting their guests, the prince and princess retired to change clothes and leave for their honeymoon aboard the royal yacht. Princess Grace removed her famous wedding dress, its important role complete. The suit she changed into was also the product of a famous American costume designer: When Edith Head had learned she could not make the wedding dress for her friend, she had insisted on making her going-away outfit, a light gray silk suit and white coat worn with a small white hat and white gloves. The prince, now dressed in a dark double-breasted jacket, accompanied his bride and her faithful poodle through the waving and cheering crowds onto the yacht, and shortly after five they were off on a restful and private month-long honeymoon.

The details of the going-away outfit and the honeymoon did not occupy the public or press, however. Although the press release two days before had finally given specific information about the wedding dress, it had merely served to whet the appetites of those eager to see the celebrated actress in her romantic bridal role. After all the secrecy and speculation, the famous bride and her mysterious wedding gown had finally been seen. Reactions to both were for the most part glowing. *The Philadelphia Inquirer* said the bride was "truly beautiful, both at a distance and close up." *The Syracuse Herald-Journal*, before describing the bride's dress, commented, "Her manner made driven snow look unchaste." An Associated Press report noted: "Grace was gorgeous, her attire setting off to perfection her classic blonde features and lithe figure. . . . The bride looked serenely regal and serious as she entered the cathedral." In an amazing metaphor, one reporter described the train as flowing "like a river of whipped cream along the plush red floor," when the bride was kneeling. A rare sour note was sounded by columnist Ilka Chase, who wrote, "Her bridal gown was, in effect, an extremely tony shirtwaist and skirt—a charming dress but not a superb one." Most, however, agreed that the gown was magnificent. Continuing the idea of a rivalry between European and American clothing in Monaco, the *New York Times* succinctly described the striking bridal attire as "the loveliest example of the American product."

The royal wedding was watched on television by an estimated thirty million Europeans. Television film was rushed to the United States through the combined efforts of a helicopter to Nice, a jet fighter to Paris, and a Trans World Airliner to New York. In addition to the television coverage, newspapers and magazines devoted an enormous amount of ink to the wedding. The following month, for those still wishing to bask in every detail, MGM released its color documentary, *The Wedding in Monaco*, which was touted as the "only complete coverage of this historic event."

After the Wedding

On the day of the wedding in Monaco, Philadelphia's *Bulletin* advertised their forthcoming June bridal issue by noting, "The Grace Kelly–Prince Rainier nuptials, and the great show of fashion finery which accompanied them, will be reflected in renewed interest in the really exquisite wedding this season." The June issue's theme was, appropriately enough, "Every Girl a Princess on Her Wedding Day."

That same day, even as the famous wedding was taking place, *Women's Wear Daily* reported that New York had caught "Monaco Bridal Fever," with Grace Kelly's bridal dress already being copied, presumably using the sketches and description released on April 17. At least ten bridal fashion firms were said to have included a version of the wedding dress, priced between $49.75 and $139.75, in their lines. By April 20, the *Philadelphia Inquirer* observed that the wedding gown was already being "copied, re-copied, and over-copied." Due to the Kelly family's warning against any kind of Princess Grace labeling, however, "Bridal shoppers will need to detect for themselves the Helen Rose influence in high-necked and long-sleeved gowns with lace bodices and wind-swept trains." Even those who did not try to imitate the well-known bridal gown were strongly influenced by the "ladylike, covered-up look" of the dress. Wedding fashions in the following months also reflected the princess's full, trained skirt, lace-trimmed veil, and crownlike headpiece, sometimes called a "Grace Kelly crown." In addition, the wedding was seen as putting the stamp of royal approval on certain bridal trends, including short dresses for flower girls and short white gloves for all members of the wedding party.

In addition to the effect on bridal wear, Grace Kelly's wedding dress and wardrobe had international fashion ramifications. While American designers basked in the publicity that Grace Kelly had brought them, Parisian designers were said to have been dealt a "stunning blow" by the preference of the bride and her entourage for American clothes. When former president Harry Truman's daughter Margaret, who was married quietly just two days after the wedding in Monaco, selected a wedding gown done in Rome rather than Paris, French designers were described as having suffered "an uppercut when they already were down on one knee—and not to pin up hems either." French couture houses were reported to be "desperately thinking up ways and means to regain the initiative and retrieve the prestige lost at Monaco." The public relations representative of the large fashion house Maison Paquin explained: "The wedding was worth a fortune in publicity to everybody but us. . . . We lost a golden opportunity."

Princess Grace and her new husband board the prince's yacht for "a month-long cruise away from the eyes of curious landlubbers." Carrying her poodle just as she did during her arrival in Monaco only a week before, the princess waves a white-gloved hand to her new subjects, well-wishers, and ever-present photographers. Prince Rainier has exchanged his splendid wedding tunic for a casual blazer, while the princess has donned her going-away outfit. The light gray suit, white coat, and close-fitting white hat were designed by her good friend and costume designer Edith Head. A nine-member crew and twelve pieces of luggage, most of them still marked with a big K for Kelly, accompanied the royal couple aboard the yacht.

The Wedding Dress at the Museum

During the buildup to the wedding and in the midst of the great interest and excitement about the bridal gown, it was announced in mid-March that Grace Kelly would give her dress to the Philadelphia Museum of Art. Many people in her hometown had been extremely proud of Miss Kelly when she became a celebrated movie star; upon her engagement to Prince Rainier in early January, they had envisioned a royal wedding at her church in Philadelphia. When the site of the nuptials was finally resolved, and it was determined the ceremony would be in Monaco, Miss Kelly's Philadelphia friends and admirers, "basking happily in reflected glory," had wished the beautiful bride well but had heaved a wistful sigh at what might have been. The announcement that she would give her wedding gown to the Museum, however, helped assuage their disappointment, as Philadelphians would "not have to depend only on pictures to see this magnificent creation, probably the most famous bridal dress of the century."

The donation of Miss Kelly's wedding dress was arranged by Henri Marceau, director of the Museum, and Esther Cole Richardson, a member of the Museum's board of trustees and also of the Philadelphia Fashion Group. Made up of women involved in fields allied to fashion, the group sought to foster interest in the arts and fashion; since 1947, they had sponsored the Museum's Fashion Wing, where two centuries of costumes from the collection were displayed. On February 23, Marceau wrote to Grace Kelly's mother to ask if he and Mrs. Richardson, permanent chairman of the Fashion Wing Committee and also an old friend of the Kellys, could call on her to discuss "an interesting idea that we have come up with." At this meeting in the Kellys' East Falls home, their idea was backed by Mrs. Kelly, and she wrote to her daughter in California. Miss Kelly, certainly well acquainted with the Museum from childhood visits, had been a guest at the Museum during Philadelphia Arts Week the previous year; under Augustus Saint-Gaudens's famed sculpture of Diana, she had received an award for bringing "glory to Philadelphia" through her preeminence in the arts. Perhaps wishing to somehow include her hometown in her wedding festivities, she quickly agreed to give her gown to the Museum.

"It is like having a part of the wedding right in Philadelphia," Mrs. Richardson said. "Grace has so many friends who wish her well, and who can't possibly go to the wedding, that we are all thrilled at having this royal wedding gown as a special gift from our princess." The Museum promised to place her bridal gown—whose design was still shrouded in secrecy—on exhibition as soon as possible after the wedding. While Miss Kelly was reported to be honored at having her wedding gown included in the Museum's collection, one condition was attached to the gift: the Museum agreed to lend the gown back to the princess "if ever a daughter may want to be married in it."

R. Sturgis Ingersoll, president of the Museum at that time, voiced his pleasure that the gown would be given to the Museum, where it could be shown to Grace Kelly's fellow Philadelphians. When he met Helen Rose in Philadelphia before the wedding, he added: "We at the Museum know so well that there are many worlds of art besides painting and sculpture, and that the art of dress is one of the most important ones. We are happy that this masterwork by you, Miss Rose, will be joining our other works of art."

Princess Grace's wedding dress was sent to Philadelphia soon after the wedding, and on May 9, Henri Marceau picked up the dress from the Kelly house so it could be prepared for exhibition. The dress would be displayed on one of the mannequins that Mary Brosnan Studios had recently modeled after Grace Kelly. Gimbel Brothers had purchased one of these mannequins and used it in a January fashion show in Philadelphia to display a replica of a dress worn on screen by Grace Kelly; when it was announced that her famous wedding dress would be coming to the Museum, the department store donated this mannequin at the behest of the Philadelphia Fashion Group. The "lifelike" mannequin had an uplifted head with painted features, including brown brows, blue eyes, red lips, three-dimensional black eyelashes, and a shiny, golden blonde wig styled in a soft, classic French twist, a style closely associated with the actress.

Published in Philadelphia's Daily News *on June 5, 1956, these photographs, taken in one of the Museum's executive offices, reflect the intense excitement over the acquisition of the wedding gown of Her Serene Highness Princess Grace of Monaco. Before going on public view, the dress and accessories were put on a mannequin created the previous winter in the likeness of then-actress Grace Kelly. Top: A young Museum employee gazes wistfully at the storybook wedding gown. Bottom: Two of the Museum's art handlers gingerly move the dressed mannequin to install it for the official welcoming ceremony.*

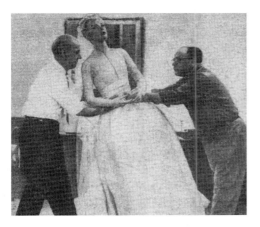

The mannequin, while modeled after the actress, was not a perfect match for her wedding dress.
While its height at 5 feet 5 1/2 inches was workable, its waist was a problem. Although the 23-inch waist
was probably very close to the actress's measurements when the mannequin was made, by the time of
the wedding she had lost weight and her wedding dress measured slightly less than 21 inches at the
waist. "I guess brides always lose weight before the wedding," said an unnamed Museum official. "We
were glad there were 2 inches of material to let out." Whatever enlarging of the waist was done to the
dress to make it fit the mannequin was concealed by the cummerbund, on which the buttons were
moved. While these adjustments caused a slight delay in the installation, they would unfortunately have
longer-lasting effects on the dress itself.

Once on the mannequin, the wedding dress was installed just inside the Museum's West Entrance
on a raised oval platform covered in red velvet and surrounded by flowers and plants, spotlights, and a
brass railing to keep the curious from getting too close. The mannequin displayed not only the gown
but also the cap, veil, prayer book, and shoes that the princess had graciously donated. A plastic bouquet
filled in for the real lilies of the valley that had been left at the church of Sainte Dévote.

Princess Grace's wedding dress was formally presented to the Museum and the public at a champagne gala at the Museum on June 4, 1956. The bride's parents were guests of honor at the occasion,
where more than five hundred guests were in attendance for what the *Bulletin* called "one of the most
glamorous and poignant occasions of the Museum's colorful history—the 'coming home' party of the
wedding gown." Mrs. Kelly, wearing a cinnamon beige afternoon dress and hat that she had worn during
the wedding festivities in Monaco, made the formal presentation. "This is one of the greatest honors in
the long list of honors which have been given the Kelly family," she said. "It is wonderful to think that
this great Philadelphia Museum would want this dress for the Fashion Wing—and even more wonderful
to think that all the people of Philadelphia are so interested in the gown which I consider my daughter's
greatest costume for her greatest role."

The wedding gown of Philadelphia's "favorite child" was now regarded, as Philadelphia's *Daily News*
put it, as "public property." It immediately proved to be a great public attraction. In the first twelve days
the "glamorous bit of history" was on exhibition, 15,125 visitors were reported. The Museum was not

The champagne gala presentation on June 4, 1956, was attended by more than five hundred fashion authorities, clothing designers, prominent Philadelphians and visitors, and members and friends of the Kelly family. Inside the west entrance of the Museum, guests gather around the wedding gown, installed on an oval platform covered in red carpet. While men wore business suits instead of the tailcoats that had been de rigueur for wedding guests in Monaco, "the room was filled with beautiful women, beautifully gowned." Many women wore styles reminiscent of those seen at the celebrated nuptials, including all manner of fashionable hats and mink stoles.

yet air conditioned, so an intense heat wave kept the crowds away during the second week, but "as soon as it cooled off a little Sunday, 1,895 people flocked in to see the dress. Most of them, naturally, were women." Their enthusiasm was said to know no bounds: "Ladies appeared on foot, by taxi, private car, and chartered bus. Many just went into the west entrance to see the gown in the reception room, gave it a full inspection and turned around and went right out again, completely ignoring the priceless treasures on the floors above gathered from the four corners of the world." Visitors came on tour buses and in school groups, and many fashion design students were observed sketching the dress. For the month Princess Grace's dress was displayed, the total visitor numbers to the Museum more than doubled.

In early July, Princess Grace's wedding gown was moved to its new home in the Museum's Fashion Wing. There, the famous dress took its place in the notable collection of gowns from the eighteenth, nineteenth, and twentieth centuries displayed in three large galleries. Princess Grace's famous dress became the finale—traditionally a bridal gown—of this historic fashion show.

On October 26, 1956, during a much-reported two-month trip to the United States, Princess Grace and Prince Rainier, accompanied by Mrs. Kelly, visited the Museum. After a luncheon, they "spent several minutes gazing at the glass showcase" that displayed her wedding dress. The princess, visibly pregnant with her first child, commented to her mother that there were not enough petticoats under the skirt to give it the bell shape, which was, she said, the whole idea of the skirt. To ensure it could be correctly arranged, Mrs. Kelly sent the Museum photographs of the dress as worn by the bride.

During the late 1950s and into the mid-1960s, the dress continued to attract many visitors. In April 1963, Princess Grace was again at the Museum, this time to receive the Crystal Award from the Philadelphia Fashion Group in recognition of her "continuing impact on the world of fashion through the years." Begun in 1957, the Crystal Ball was held every two years at the Museum; the 1963 theme, "Philadelphia Greats," honored other successful Philadelphia natives, including famed contralto Marion Anderson, singer Eddie Fisher, and designers James Galanos and Gustave Tassell. The princess, her Hollywood glamour "enhanced now with international overtones," wore a deep blue silk organdy gown with an asymmetrical ruffle skirt by Balenciaga that was set off by diamonds and a towering chignon. A special temporary display set up in her honor featured a dress worn by Grace Kelly in *The Swan* that Helen Rose had lent for the occasion, and it also included the dresses of her matron of honor and a flower girl, lent by Grace Kelly's mother, and a bridesmaid dress, lent by Maree Frisby Pamp. While the bridal attendants' clothing was on view only for a short time in 1963, all were subsequently donated to the Museum.

In May 1966, Princess Grace's wedding dress was temporarily removed from the Fashion Wing to take pride of place in a special exhibition of wedding fashions called *The Bride in Fashion*. Thirty examples of matrimonial gowns from the eighteenth through twentieth centuries were displayed in the Museum's Great Stair Hall on wire forms, while the royal wedding dress was shown on the balcony at the top of the stairs on its mannequin. The exhibition proved to be extremely popular and was extended through July. The *Bulletin* also noted that Princess Grace's dress had been a major attraction throughout the past decade and that picture postcards of this object outsold all others at the Museum.

By the early 1970s, although the Fashion Wing had been temporarily closed several times for refurbishment, Princess Grace's gown—still said to be the Museum's most popular attraction—was always returned to its place as the "crowning glory" of the costume galleries. In April 1975, however, the Fashion Wing, along with much of the Museum, was closed to allow for the installation of climate control, an addition that would prevent fluctuations in humidity and temperature harmful to many works of art, including textiles. During this major project, many of the Museum's galleries were reconfigured. While the rest of the Museum reopened in 1976, it was not until September 1979 that the new fashion galleries had their grand reopening, and once again Princess Grace's famous wedding dress was featured, albeit briefly.

Shortly after the new galleries opened, the wedding gown and accessories were removed from public display for conservation reasons. By this time, museum practices and policies regarding the display and care of costume were evolving. Research had proved that exposing textiles to high or constant light for long periods of time could be extremely damaging; to preserve the wedding dress and accessories, they were stored in complete darkness. While Museum officials explained the reasons for the "retirement," public demand to see the much-loved dress meant it was not done without causing "a great hue and cry." In April 1981, to commemorate the twenty-fifth anniversary of the royal wedding, Princess Grace's wedding gown was displayed for two weeks in the Museum's Great Stair Hall.

When the Fashion Wing closed in 1983, the Costume and Textiles Department refocused its efforts on special exhibitions and installations. In 1993, the major exhibition *Ahead of Fashion: Hats of the Twentieth Century*, included Princess Grace's wedding headdress. Now displayed in a low case, visitors could closely examine its delicate lace roses, wax orange blossoms, and seed pearls.

Top: In early July 1956, the dress was moved to its new home in the Museum's Fashion Wing, where it became the culmination of the display of two centuries from the collection. Inaugurated in 1947, the Fashion Wing showcased historic costume and contemporary apparel through roomlike tableaux in "show-window fashion." Here, the dramatic evolution of feminine style from the early to mid-twentieth century can be seen; a 1953 gold net crinolined dress and fox fur muff by Anne Fogarty precedes Grace Kelly's wedding dress, which was visible from all three fashion galleries.

Bottom: During their first trip to the United States since their marriage, Prince Rainier and Princess Grace visited the Museum on October 26, 1956, and inspected the dress that had played such a central role in their fairy-tale wedding six months before. Princess Grace wears a tailored maternity suit and reptile-skin pumps, carried a large handbag and white gloves, and sported a favorite pink fur felt hat from a milliner in Monte Carlo that received a lot of attention during this trip. Princess Grace continued to be a leader of fashion in some areas even after her marriage; she was said to have done more for the millinery business than any other woman in the previous twenty years.

Although the headdress's relatively good condition allowed it to be displayed, other parts of Princess Grace's wedding ensemble had been more severely affected by many years of nearly continuous exhibition. The gown's bodice, made of delicate lace, had been put under some stress by the slightly too large shoulders, arms, and torso of the original mannequin, and years of light exposure had also had a deleterious effect. Furthermore, the materials used for the beautiful gown, constructed with such care at MGM, had not been chosen with longevity in mind. Under the skirt, some of the petticoats and supports had been stiffened with nonwoven synthetic interfacing, and the acids in this fabric had caused it to become brittle and yellowed. Even natural fibers like silk, however, are not immune to decay; the very sheer silk tulle of the veil had withstood only a few years under bright exhibition lights before deterioration began to show, and another veil with less delicate lace edging had been displayed with the dress since at least the mid-1970s. While the silk faille of the outer skirt was fairly sturdy, the thin silk taffeta used for the smoothing layer of the underskirt had been weighted to give it more body; this process, done since the late nineteenth century, involved impregnating the fibers with metallic salts, which over time cause the woven structure to break down irreversibly. In addition, early attempts to clean the dress, while well meaning, had been carried out in the years before the effects of detergents were scientifically studied and their effects understood. Thus, by the mid-1990s, Princess Grace's wedding gown was in need of conservation to ensure its preservation and enable it to be displayed in short-term special exhibitions.

In 1956 and for several decades thereafter, Grace Kelly's wedding dress was displayed on a mannequin modeled to look like the actress, with painted features and a blond synthetic wig. This postcard of the dress on display in the Museum's Fashion Wing shows how clearly the actress's face would have been seen through the veil. The veil is adorned only around the circular edge by lace decoration of delicate flowers and sprays of wheat; the motifs are deepest around the front and gradually get shallower as they encircle the back.

In 1995, in preparation for an exhibition of highlights from the Costume and Textiles collection, the Women's Committee of the Museum provided funding that allowed the time-consuming conservation of the dress to be undertaken. Trained personnel documented every step, ran appropriate tests, and utilized methods and materials that would stabilize the gown yet be fully reversible in the future. Since the silk tulle of the original veil had deteriorated to a point where it could not be conserved, the veil was restored by carefully detaching the delicate lace edging, motifs, and seed pearls from the disintegrated tulle and stitching them to a replacement layer of silk tulle.

The newly conserved dress, although still fragile, was stable enough to be lent to two exhibitions in Europe. In early 1996, the gown was installed as the centerpiece of a display of bridal fashions at Printemps in Paris, and in the winter of 1996–97, it was sent to Rome for the exhibition *Il Principato di Monaco: Settecento Anni di Storia, 1297–1997*. Held at the Palazzo Venezia, the exhibition, mounted at the behest of Prince Rainier, focused on the history of Monaco, with the wedding dress highlighting an important moment in Monégasque history; both Prince Rainier and Prince Albert attended the gala opening of the exhibition.

In 1997, planning for the survey exhibition that fall, *Best Dressed: 250 Years of Style,* accelerated. Princess Grace's wedding dress, together with the dresses of her bridesmaid and flower girl, would be displayed on a high platform at the apex of the space, set against a large photograph of the outside of the

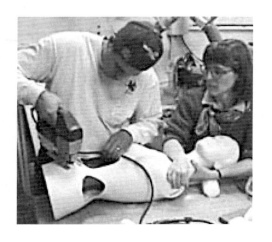

cathedral on her wedding day. While the small mannequin used for the two European exhibitions had properly supported and not strained the dress, it had failed to capture the elegant carriage for which Grace Kelly was famous. For the Museum's exhibition, it was decided that the famous wedding dress would need a new mannequin—one that, like others in the exhibition, would focus attention on the dress. Modern museum practices require that a mount be altered to fit the object rather than the reverse, so it proved necessary to specially reconstruct a mannequin to make it suitable for the dress. Paper hair was added to replicate the bride's large chignon, and the entire mannequin was painted a neutral color to give a sculptural look. *Best Dressed*, on view from October 21, 1997, to January 4, 1998, attracted more than 125,000 visitors eager to see the treasures from the Museum's Costume and Textiles collection, including, of course, the wedding gown donated over forty years before by Her Serene Highness Princess Grace of Monaco.

The Museum now balances the obligation to provide the public with opportunities to see the famous dress with the need to preserve it. To celebrate the fiftieth anniversary of the wedding of Grace Kelly and Prince Rainier, the dress will once again be on view for a limited time in the spring of 2006, giving old admirers and a new generation the rare opportunity to see this piece of fashion, film, and royal history.

Continuing Influence

The bridal gown Grace Kelly wore so gracefully at her wedding in Monaco, viewed in person by thousands and seen in photographs by millions, has had a great influence on popular conceptions of bridal elegance from that day to this. Although in the ensuing decades, bridal attire has evolved with changes in fashion and society, Grace Kelly continues to emplify the elegant, fairy-tale bride. Many elements of her wedding attire—delicate pearl-bedecked lace, an extravagantly full, trained skirt, a gracefully flowing veil, and a crownlike cap—are still considered the ultimate in romantic bridal fashion.

After her marriage, Grace Kelly, as many still referred to her, continued to be hailed as an icon of style in fields other than wedding wear. Shortly after the wedding, fashion authority Lilly Daché stated that Grace Kelly was "the perfect symbol of glamour for our time," uniting as she did the six elements considered important in 1956: breeding, reserved sex appeal, perfect grooming, quiet good taste, slenderness, and femininity combined with independence. The fashion influence of the Grace Kelly Look also lingered after the wedding. In September 1956, a Boston department store reported that it had been inundated with hundreds of demands for the star's infamous debarkation hat shaped "like an inverted soup bowl." When the new princess took a "monster-sized" handbag on her honeymoon, copies of these were reported to be selling like hotcakes in London; in due time, she became associated with the Hermès bag she sometimes carried and gave her name to this status symbol. Princess Grace was inducted to the Fashion Hall of Fame in 1960, but soon the clothes she wore as a wife, mother, and princess, while often elegant, had little influence on fashion as it moved on to emphasize youthful energy rather than well-groomed, ladylike restraint. With her marriage, Grace Kelly left her film career behind; as princess of Monaco, she devoted herself to raising her three children and fulfilling her duty to her husband and adopted country until her life was cut tragically short in September 1982.

Film preserves actress Grace Kelly's on-screen beauty and style; off screen, the classic American style she exemplified and the Grace Kelly Look she inspired perfectly captured the mood of the 1950s, while her personal wardrobe, bridal trousseau, and wedding dress beautifully illustrated the nature and quality of midcentury American fashion. Fifty years later, Grace Kelly's name continues to be evoked as the quintessential fairy-tale bride and whenever understated elegance is mentioned.

Opposite: In 1997, in preparation for an exhibition highlighting the treasures of the Museum's costume collection, Princess Grace's newly conserved wedding dress was fitted with a new mannequin that would not place any stress on the delicate fabric. To this end, the graceful head of one mannequin was joined to the smaller torso of another; even then, with curatorial guidance, Museum construction staff had to cut away much of the mannequin's fiberglass waist to make it fit the less than 21-inch waist of the gown. The waist was then filled in with conservationally approved structural foam to provide proper support for the fragile dress.

Top right: *Best Dressed: 250 Years of Style* featured Princess Grace's wedding gown flanked by the dresses of a bridesmaid and a flower girl. The royal bridal party was installed at the apex of a large, open special exhibition gallery; while they were placed on the same high, stepped platforms used to showcase the other gala ensembles shown in the exhibition, the special group was distinguished by massive columns framing a large photographic background of the princess arriving at the Monégasque cathedral steps on her wedding day.

Bottom right: Prior to her wedding, Grace Kelly had agreed to donate her dress to the Museum so it could be enjoyed by her fellow Philadelphians and visitors from around the world. When she made that promise, the dress had been seen only by the bride and its creators; on April 19, 1956, it became one of the best-known wedding gowns in history. Those who saw it that day and in displays and special exhibitions in the decades since have generally agreed that the gown perfectly reflects the beauty, style, and elegance for which Grace Kelly is known.

THE CONSTRUCTION OF THE WEDDING DRESS

Grace Kelly's wedding dress consists of four parts and is constructed in a very unusual way, for its underpinnings were not created as separate pieces but instead were built into the lace bodice and the silk faille skirt. Since ease and speed of dressing would not have dictated this composite construction, it might have been done so that the underpinnings could not shift during wear. Whatever the reason, since the bodice and the skirt each include several disparate layers, their construction is extremely complex. The train insert and cummerbund, although less complicated, were also engineered to give the desired shape and style.

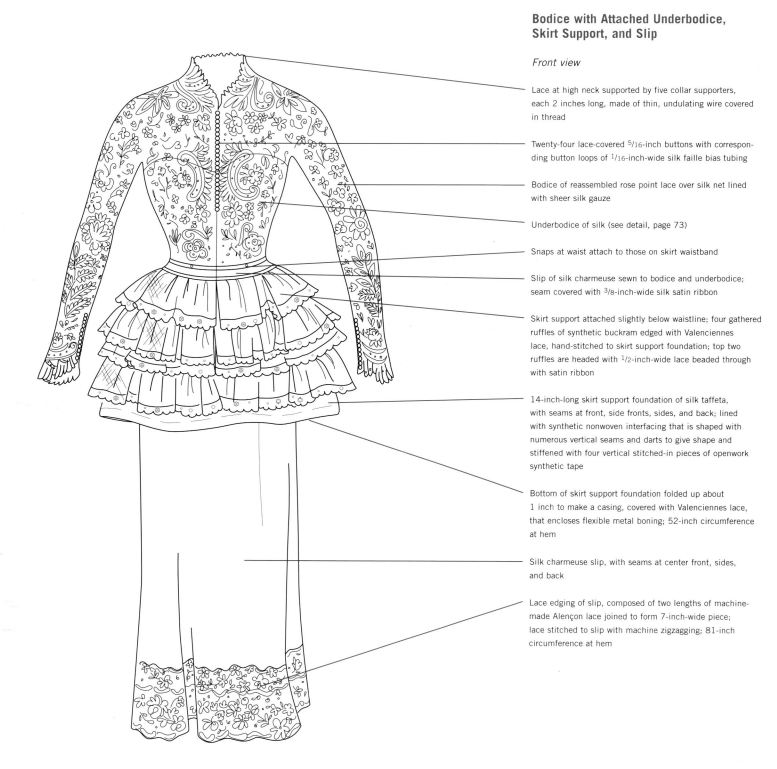

Bodice with Attached Underbodice, Skirt Support, and Slip

Front view

Lace at high neck supported by five collar supporters, each 2 inches long, made of thin, undulating wire covered in thread

Twenty-four lace-covered 5/16-inch buttons with corresponding button loops of 1/16-inch-wide silk faille bias tubing

Bodice of reassembled rose point lace over silk net lined with sheer silk gauze

Underbodice of silk (see detail, page 73)

Snaps at waist attach to those on skirt waistband

Slip of silk charmeuse sewn to bodice and underbodice; seam covered with 3/8-inch-wide silk satin ribbon

Skirt support attached slightly below waistline; four gathered ruffles of synthetic buckram edged with Valenciennes lace, hand-stitched to skirt support foundation; top two ruffles are headed with 1/2-inch-wide lace beaded through with satin ribbon

14-inch-long skirt support foundation of silk taffeta, with seams at front, side fronts, sides, and back; lined with synthetic nonwoven interfacing that is shaped with numerous vertical seams and darts to give shape and stiffened with four vertical stitched-in pieces of openwork synthetic tape

Bottom of skirt support foundation folded up about 1 inch to make a casing, covered with Valenciennes lace, that encloses flexible metal boning; 52-inch circumference at hem

Silk charmeuse slip, with seams at center front, sides, and back

Lace edging of slip, composed of two lengths of machine-made Alençon lace joined to form 7-inch-wide piece; lace stitched to slip with machine zigzagging; 81-inch circumference at hem

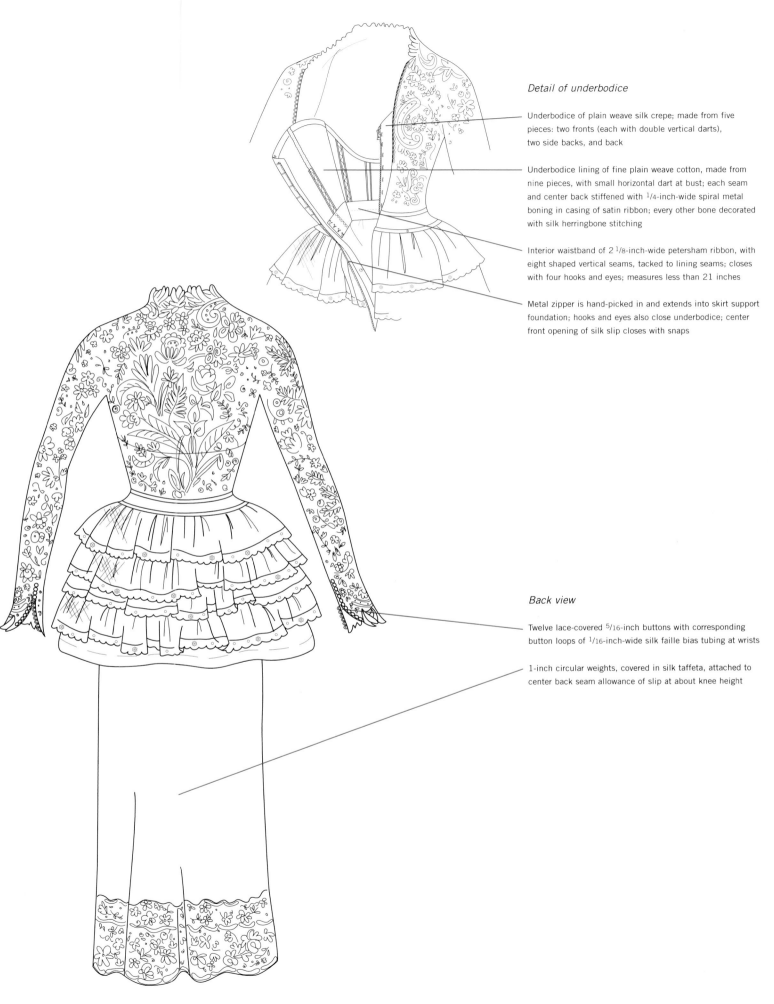

Detail of underbodice

Underbodice of plain weave silk crepe; made from five pieces: two fronts (each with double vertical darts), two side backs, and back

Underbodice lining of fine plain weave cotton, made from nine pieces, with small horizontal dart at bust; each seam and center back stiffened with $1/4$-inch-wide spiral metal boning in casing of satin ribbon; every other bone decorated with silk herringbone stitching

Interior waistband of $2 1/8$-inch-wide petersham ribbon, with eight shaped vertical seams, tacked to lining seams; closes with four hooks and eyes; measures less than 21 inches

Metal zipper is hand-picked in and extends into skirt support foundation; hooks and eyes also close underbodice; center front opening of silk slip closes with snaps

Back view

Twelve lace-covered $5/16$-inch buttons with corresponding button loops of $1/16$-inch-wide silk faille bias tubing at wrists

1-inch circular weights, covered in silk taffeta, attached to center back seam allowance of slip at about knee height

Cummerbund

Top view

Silk faille cut on the bias forms four soft, irregular downward pleats; measures 24 1/2 inches across (including flange for closure), 5 7/8 inches high at center front, and 3 3/4 inches high at center back ends

Center back closure, probably originally of six or seven silk faille–covered 1/2-inch buttons and corresponding silk faille loops (buttons now removed but six preserved, missing loops reconstructed here)

Interior view

Silk faille folded to inside 3/4 inch at top, bottom, and button end over silk taffeta lining; fabric at loop end folded back 2 1/2 inches to form closure flange, 1/2-inch-wide Valenciennes lace finishes hem edges

Eight metal bones of graduated lengths in silk satin ribbon casings extend to top and bottom edges under hem (bones at center backs concealed under lace)

Five hooks remaining from original closure (corresponding eyes missing)

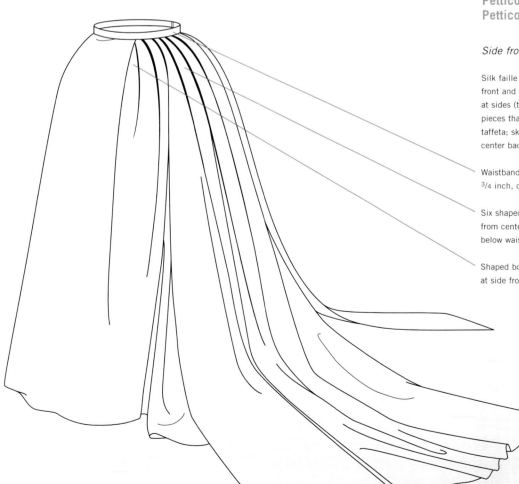

Skirt with Smoothing Petticoat, Ruffled Petticoat, and Attached Foundation Petticoat

Side front view

Silk faille skirt made with seven pieces: one piece for front and sides, gored side backs with extra gores attached at sides (these do not extend to waistband), and gored back pieces that extend to form train; back pieces lined in silk taffeta; skirt front length is 44 1/4 inches; skirt length at center back opening is 73 3/4 inches

Waistband circumference is 22 3/4 inches and height is 3/4 inch, closed at center back with two hooks and eyes

Six shaped overlapping pleats at each side back pleated out from center back and stitched down for 3/4 inch to 1 inch below waistband

Shaped box pleat across center front; overlaps deep pleat at side fronts that is pleated out from center back

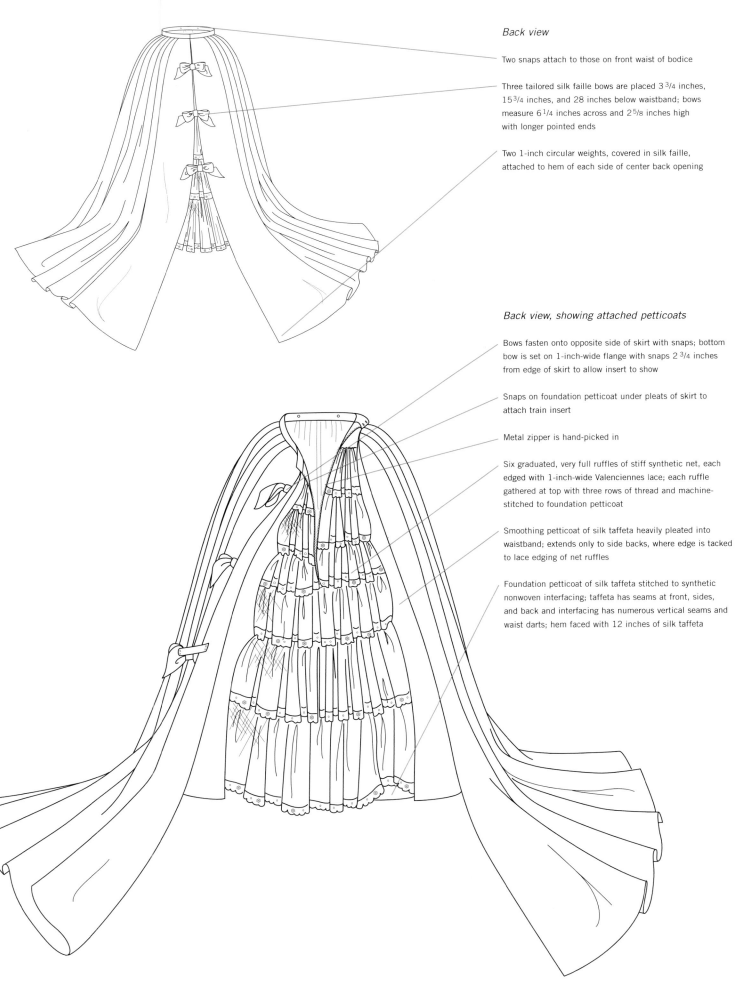

Back view

Two snaps attach to those on front waist of bodice

Three tailored silk faille bows are placed 3 3/4 inches, 15 3/4 inches, and 28 inches below waistband; bows measure 6 1/4 inches across and 2 5/8 inches high with longer pointed ends

Two 1-inch circular weights, covered in silk faille, attached to hem of each side of center back opening

Back view, showing attached petticoats

Bows fasten onto opposite side of skirt with snaps; bottom bow is set on 1-inch-wide flange with snaps 2 3/4 inches from edge of skirt to allow insert to show

Snaps on foundation petticoat under pleats of skirt to attach train insert

Metal zipper is hand-picked in

Six graduated, very full ruffles of stiff synthetic net, each edged with 1-inch-wide Valenciennes lace; each ruffle gathered at top with three rows of thread and machine-stitched to foundation petticoat

Smoothing petticoat of silk taffeta heavily pleated into waistband; extends only to side backs, where edge is tacked to lace edging of net ruffles

Foundation petticoat of silk taffeta stitched to synthetic nonwoven interfacing; taffeta has seams at front, sides, and back and interfacing has numerous vertical seams and waist darts; hem faced with 12 inches of silk taffeta

Train Insert

Top view

Shown spread out flat; when worn, falls in soft vertical folds, with only triangle with lace appliqué showing; made of two layers of silk tulle over silk taffeta foundation with synthetic net ruffles; center back length is 74 1/2 inches

Both layers of tulle gathered to form 4 1/4-inch-wide top placket, taffeta foundation layer pleated into same; top of placket edged with silk satin ribbon

Top layer of tulle appliquéd with lace motifs in triangular pattern of central stem of flowers surrounded by floral sprigs; appliqué area measures 32 inches at bottom and extends 34 1/2 inches up from hem

Edge of top tulle layer finished with scalloped lace

Bottom net ruffle finished with scalloped lace

Top view showing underlayers

Snaps to attach placket to skirt back below waist

Foundation layer of silk taffeta, with center back seam, heavily pleated into top placket

Second layer of tulle unadorned, unhemmed, slightly shorter than top layer

Four very full ruffles of stiff synthetic net, stitched onto taffeta foundation with machine zigzagging (only three ruffles are visible since deep middle ruffle covers narrower ruffle underneath)

Net ruffles swing-tacked to each other at several points to keep them in place

Three sets of three circular 1 1/4-inch weights encased in silk near hem of taffeta foundation; one set attached vertically along center back seam, others on each side parallel to hem

Bottom net ruffle finished with scalloped lace that has been hand-stitched on

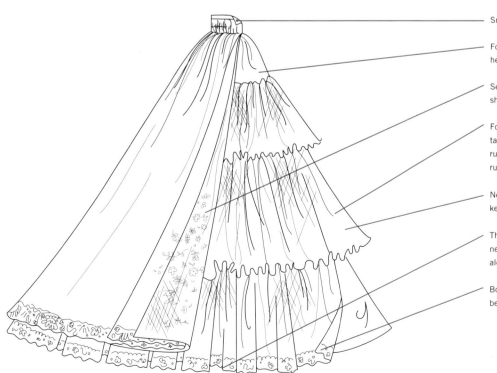

ACKNOWLEDGMENTS

PRINCESS GRACE'S WEDDING DRESS has been well known and well loved for decades; I am most grateful for the opportunity to explore the context behind this famous piece of cultural history. My thanks to Director Anne d'Harnoncourt, who conceived the idea of the book and gave it her insightful support. I offer my ardent thanks to Sherry Babbitt, who kept everything on track with utmost dedication, to Beth Huseman, whose editorial expertise, good humor, and fight-to-the-death standards made working together a true pleasure, and to Andrea Hemmann, who created the book's beautiful design. Thanks to the Costume and Textiles staff, especially Joanna Fulginiti for her invaluable, skillful, and cheerful help with images, charts, citations, and so much more, and to Dilys Blum, Monica Brown, Carol Rossi, and Meg Jacovino, as well as to Sara Reiter in Textile Conservation.

Many others at the Museum also helped make this book possible, including, in the Library, Visual Resources, and Archives, Lilah Mittelstaedt, who handled my many interlibrary loans, and Evan Towle, Lynn Rosenthal, Susan Anderson, and Bertha Adams. Thanks also to Conna Clark and Jason Wierzbicki in Rights and Reproductions, Graydon Wood and Andrea Simon in Photography, Joe Mikuliak, photographer in Conservation, and Rich Bonk and Kathleen Krattenmaker in Publishing. Both this book and the exhibition also benefited greatly from the excellent work of those in Development, Marketing and Public Relations, Special Exhibitions, Education, Audio-Visual, Information Services, and Installations.

Several devoted volunteers provided much-appreciated research assistance; thanks especially to Lindsay Friedman, who devoted part of her summer to perusing microfilm of Philadelphia newspapers, Rebecca Matheson for her help with *Women's Wear Daily*, and Muriel Peters. My thanks also to our other departmental volunteers, including Nancy Bergman, Ingrid Johnson, and Dean Ockert.

Finally, I am sincerely grateful to my friends, colleagues, and Bill Gannotta, who kept me going during my time in Graceland.

H. Kristina Haugland

SOURCE NOTES

Captions

p. 8 a reserved child: Mrs. John B. Kelly (ghostwritten), "Grace Walked to Dance With Her First Date When She Was 13, Her Mother Remembers," *Evening Bulletin* (Philadelphia), January 16, 1956; **p. 9** "no oomph, no cheesecake": "The Girl in White Gloves," *Time*, January 31, 1955, p. 47; **p. 10** "an interesting blonde": Advertisement in *Van Wert* (Ohio) *Times-Bulletin*, November 12, 1953; **p. 10** "ticket to Stardustown": Walter Winchell, "On Broadway," *Nevada State Journal*, December 10, 1954; **p. 10** "glamorous, beautiful": Pete Martin, "The Luckiest Girl in Hollywood," *Saturday Evening Post*, October 30, 1954, p. 58; **p. 12** "If I can't do": Phyllis Battelle (INS), "Grace Kelly Gets Exactly What She Wants," *Lima* (Ohio) *News*, April 4, 1955; **p. 12** "flatness of voice": N.A., "Bing Crosby Hits Heights In Keith's 'The Country Girl,'" *Syracuse* (N.Y.) *Post-Standard*, March 31, 1955; **p. 13** "a triumph of perfect": "Exciting Star Duo in Hitchcock Thrill Film 'To Catch a Thief,' Opens At 'New Ames' Theatre Wednesday," *Ames* (Iowa) *Daily Tribune*, September 17, 1955; **p. 13** "one of the most gorgeous": R.I.S., "Her Beauty, Acting Save Film," *Syracuse* (N.Y.) *Herald-Journal*, September 15, 1955; **p. 13** "She'll be different": Erskine Johnson (NEA), *Indiana* (Pa.) *Evening Gazette*, April 2, 1955; **p. 15** "a startling change": "The Girl in White Gloves," *Time*, January 31, 1955, p. 46; **p. 15** even press agents: Cynthia Lowry (AP), "These Women," *Van Wert* (Ohio) *Times-Bulletin*, December 10, 1954; **p. 15** Writers and gossip columnists: Erskine Johnson (NEA), "Fame Was Grace's Goal; She Reached It Fast," *Ames* (Iowa) *Daily Tribune*, November 12, 1954; **p. 15** "The thing that": Fred Coe quoted in Isabella Taves, "The Seven Graces," *McCalls*, January 1955, p. 68; **p. 17** "likes to buy new": Isabella Taves, "The Seven Graces," *McCalls*, January 1955, p. 69;

p. 17 "loyal to her old": Ibid., p. 71; **p. 17** "She selects clothes": "Kelly Is a Lady, Irish Luck? She Doesn't Need It," *Gazette and Bulletin* (Williamsport, Pa.), November 4, 1954; **p. 18** "too wholesome": "People Are Talking About . . . ," *Vogue*, March 1, 1955, p. 130; **p. 18** "short gloves to longies": North American Newspaper Alliance, "Everybody Glows At Awards Party," *Dallas Morning News*, December 13, 1955; **p. 19** "subdued eastern": *The Monessen* (Pa.) *Daily Independent*, July 23, 1954. Cassini also claimed, "I created the 'Grace Kelly look' for her; I put her in subdued, elegant dresses that set off her patrician good looks." See Oleg Cassini, *In My Own Fashion: An Autobiography* (New York: Simon and Schuster. 1987), p. 247; **p. 21** $175 beige silk dress: Cynthia Cabot, "Fabrics Tell Fashion Tale," *Philadelphia Inquirer*, January 11, 1956; **p. 21** "To Catch a Prince": Blanche Krause, "New Fashions Inspired by Ancient Greece," *Evening Bulletin* (Philadelphia), January 11, 1956; **p. 21** "by doing": United Press, "Grace Goes to California, Prince Rainier to Florida," *Sheboyan* (Wisc.) *Press*, January 7, 1956; **p. 22** "Miss Kelly Dons": "Miss Kelly Dons Wedding Gown," *Evening Bulletin* (Philadelphia), January 11, 1956; **p. 25** "a circus": United Press, "Prince Scared by U.S. Press," *Philadelphia Inquirer*, January 12, 1956; **p. 25** bridal fashion show: March 21, 1956, photograph caption courtesy of Corbis; **p. 27** put her stamp: Kittie Campbell, "The Grace Kelly Look; The T-Square Silhouette," *Sunday Bulletin* (Philadelphia), February 26, 1956; **p. 28** "walled city": Cynthia Lowry (AP), *Sunday Times Signal* (Zanesville, Ohio), April 17, 1955; **p. 28** a year's leave: United Press, "Grace Arrives in New York," *Traverse-City* (Mich.) *Record Eagle*, March 23, 1956; **p. 28** While film costumes were usually reused: Arlene C. La Rue in her column "Woman's Agenda," *Syracuse* (N.Y.) *Herald-Journal*, September 25, 1955; **p. 28** perfect for wear: Helen Rose in Fay Hammond, "Grace's Bridal Gown Has

Veil—of Secrecy," *Los Angeles Times*, April 10, 1956; **p. 29** her own packing: Gant Gaither, *Princess of Monaco: The Story of Grace Kelly* (New York: Henry Holt, 1957), p. 73; **p. 29** recent trousseau purchases: Elizabeth Bernkopf, "Grace Isn't Going to Her Prince Empty-Handed!" *Boston Daily Globe*, April 17, 1956; **p. 31** education in courtly: "And Now Here Comes The Bride," *Life*, April 9, 1956, p. 46; **p. 33** "greatest entertainment enterprise": Howard Strickling in Helen Rose, *Just Make Them Beautiful: The Many Worlds of a Designing Woman* (Santa Monica, Calif.: Dennis Landman Publishers, 1976), p. 47; **p. 33** $55 million . . . 250 different types of jobs: Lowry (AP), *Sunday Times Signal* (Zanesville, Ohio), April 17, 1955; **p. 33** "beehive of activity": Profile in the studio's employee newsletter, "Know Your Studio," *Inside MGM*, September 21, 1951; courtesy of Margaret Herrick Library, Academy of Motion Picture Arts and Sciences, Beverly Hills, California. Thanks to Kristine Krueger of the National Film Information Service for her help with MGM information and images; **p. 33** "fitters and seamstresses": Ibid.; **p. 33** "most glamorous women": Ibid.; **p. 33** "fitters and seamstresses": Rose, *Just Make Them Beautiful*, p. 105; **p. 34** "It's not what you": David Evins in *Footwear News*, quoted in Linda O'Keefe, *Shoes* (New York: Workman, 1996), pp. 210–11; **p. 36** satin shoebox: Photograph caption, "Wedding Shoes," *Dallas Morning News*, April 10, 1956; **p. 38** "the most talked-about": Ruth Holman Baker, "Joe Hung [sic] Having Fun Designing Gowns for Grace's Attendants," *Dallas Morning News*, April 1, 1956; **p. 38** not primarily interested: Ibid.; **p. 38** fairy tale: Ibid.; **p. 43** "looked like a lady": "Grace Kelly Sails in Beige Suit," *Women's Wear Daily*, April 5, 1956; **p. 43** "inevitably beige": Ibid.; **p. 43** *Harper's Bazaar*: "American Suits: Loosed Out, Squared Away," *Harper's Bazaar*, March 1956, p. 154; **p. 43** I. Magnin: "Grace Kelly Sails in Beige Suit," *Women's Wear Daily*, April 5, 1956; **p. 43** seam-

less: Ibid.; **p. 44** "stand on each": Ilka Chase, "Monte Carlo Casino Found Dull, Dreary," *Boston Daily Globe*, April 12, 1956; **p. 48** customarily made only: Rose, *Just Make Them Beautiful*, p. 63; **p. 53** what Miss Rose described: Rose, *Just Make Them Beautiful*, p. 106; **p. 54** "co-star": Blanche Krause, "Helen Rose, Designer of Grace's Gowns, Keeps the Wedding Dress Top Secret," *Evening Bulletin* (Philadelphia), April 11, 1956; **p. 54** "She's too beautiful": Bob Considine (INS), "Grace and Prince Sail Away on Honeymoon," *Syracuse* (N.Y.) *Herald-Journal*, April 19, 1956; **p. 61** "had to compete": "Noble Pair in the Palace," *Life*, May 14, 1956, p. 66; **p. 61** "princely plumage": Ibid.; **p. 62** "a month-long cruise": Considine, "Grace and Prince Sail," *Syracuse* (N.Y.) *Herald-Journal*, April 19, 1956; **p. 62** twelve pieces of: Preston Grover, "Grace and Her Prince Sail Into the Misty Sea," *Syracuse* (N.Y.) *Post-Standard*, April 20, 1956; **p. 64** Mrs. Kelly's eyes: Kittie Campbell, "Grace's Gown Given to Museum At Fashion Group Gala Event," *Evening Bulletin* (Philadelphia), June 5, 1956; **p. 65** five hundred: Ibid.; **p. 65** "the room was filled": Libby McCall, "15,125 View Wedding Gown of Princess Grace in 1st 12 Days at Museum of Art," *Cherry Hill* (N.J.) *Herald*, July 5, 1956; **p. 67** "show-window fashion": Undated Philadelphia Museum of Art press release (probably from October 10, 1947); **p. 67** favorite pink fur felt hat: United Press, "Princess Grace in New York with Husband," *Daily Courier* (Connellsville, Pa.), September 12, 1956; **p. 67** said to have done more for the millinery business: Associated Press, "Princess Grace Gives Millinery Much-Needed Boost," *Berkshire Eagle* (Pittsfield, Mass.), February 1, 1957; **p. 69** "gracious and beautiful": United Press, "Pennsylvanians Hail Princess Grace of Monaco with Bright Fashion Ball," *Camden* (N.J.) *Courier-Post*, April 23, 1963.

Text

p. 8 John Henry Kelly . . . ten children: Arthur H. Lewis, *Those Philadelphia Kellys* (New York: William Morrow, 1977), pp. 30–32; Frederick A. McCord, "That Kelly Family," *Evening Bulletin* (Philadelphia), January 9, 1956; **p. 9** John B. Kelly became: Obituary for John B. Kelly, *Philadelphia Inquirer*, June 21, 1960; Steven Englund, *Grace of Monaco: An Interpretive Biography* (Garden City, N.Y.: Doubleday, 1984), pp. 4–10; **p. 9** "Everybody said": Joe McCarthy, "The Genteel Miss Kelly," *Cosmopolitan*, April 1955, p. 30; **p. 9** personal drive: Phyllis Battelle (INS), "Grace Kelly Gets Exactly What She Wants," *Lima* (Ohio) *News*, April 4, 1955; **p. 10** fun they had choosing: Princess Grace quoted in Rose, *Just Make Them Beautiful*, p. 105; **p. 10** Hitchcock . . . closely supervised: Donald Spoto, *The Dark Side of Genius: The Life of Alfred Hitchcock* (Boston: Little, Brown, 1983), p. 343; **p. 10** "After this I": Ibid., p. 344; **p. 10** "never wears": *Rear Window*, DVD, directed by Alfred Hitchcock (1954; Hollywood, CA: Universal City Studios, 1997). See also Sarah Street, "'The Dresses Had Told Me': Fashion and Femininity in *Rear Window*," in *Alfred Hitchcock's Rear Window*, ed. John Belton (Cambridge: Cambridge University Press, 2000), pp. 91–109; **p. 10** "There was a reason": Spoto, *Dark Side of Genius*, p. 348; **pp. 10–12** "Few actresses": Edith Head and Paddy Calistro, *Edith Head's Hollywood* (New York: E. P. Dutton, 1983), pp. 108–9. See also David Chierichetti, *Edith Head: The Life and Times of Hollywood's Celebrated Costume Designer* (New York: HarperCollins, 2003), p. 126; **p. 10** conspired to resist: Princess Grace, interview by Donald Spoto (1975), in Spoto, *Dark Side of Genius*, p. 348; **p. 10** not a costume picture: Head and Calistro, *Edith Head's Hollywood*, p. 108; **p. 10** "Kelly flavoring": Pete Martin, "The Luckiest Girl in Hollywood," *Saturday Evening Post*, October 30, 1954, p. 58; **p. 10** looked truly depressed: Head and Calistro, *Edith Head's Hollywood*, p. 108; **p. 12** "It makes me so mad": "The Girl in White Gloves," *Time*, January 31, 1955, p. 51; **p. 12** "Keep right on": Martin, "The Luckiest Girl in Hollywood," p. 58; **p. 12** "where style is created": Head and Calistro, *Edith Head's Hollywood*, p. 110; **p. 12** Hermès: Gwen Robyns, *Princess Grace: A Biography* (New York: David McKay, 1976), p. 101; **p. 13** favorite film: Chierichetti, *Edith Head*, p. 128; **p. 13** "this year of Grace": "Hollywood's Hottest Property," *Life*, April 26, 1954, p. 117; **p. 13** "a tidal wave": Cynthia Lowry (AP), "These Women" *Van Wert* (Ohio) *Times-Bulletin*, December 10, 1954; **p. 13** "the latest star": *Newsweek*, May 17, 1954, p. 17; **p. 13** "the most outstanding": Aline Mosby (UP), "Grace Is Cinderella in Reverse," *Syracuse* (N.Y.) *Herald-Journal*, November 20, 1954; **p. 13** "a Main Line debutante": Martin, "The Luckiest Girl in Hollywood," p. 55; "The Girl in White Gloves," *Time*, January 31, 1955, p. 46; **p. 13** new type of actress: Vivian Brown, "American Girl Tops in Glamour," *Dixon* (Illinois) *Evening Telegraph*, December 24, 1955; **p. 13** "flatly refused": "The Girl in White Gloves," *Time*, January 31, 1955, p. 46; **p. 13** "writing about her": Martin, "The Luckiest Girl in Hollywood," p. 29; **p. 14** "Perhaps atomic": "The Kelly's Cool Film Beauty," *Newsweek*, May 17, 1954, p. 100; **p. 14** "All I'd do": "The Girl in White Gloves," *Time*, January 31, 1955, p. 50; **p. 14** "There were costumes" . . . favorite assignments: Rose, *Just Make Them Beautiful*, p. 103; **p. 14** "like an angel": Orville Prescott of the *New York Times* quoted in Walter Winchell, "On Broadway," *Zanesville* (Ohio) *Signal*, November 15, 1955; **p. 14** *Swan*-inspired fashion: Blanche Krause, "American Designers Offer You Infinite Variety for Spring," *Evening Bulletin* (Philadelphia), January 15, 1956; **p. 14** named the highest-earning: "Jimmy Stewart Voted New King of Box Office, Grace Kelly Second," *Newport Daily News*, December 29, 1955; **p. 14** something startlingly different: Mosby, "Grace Is Cinderella in Reverse"; **p. 14** "Grace wanted to": Oleg Cassini, interview by Steven Englund (April 28, 1983), in Englund, *Grace of Monaco*, p. 28; **p. 14** "Bryn Mawr look": Ibid.; **p. 14** "a dream schoolmistress": Sheilah Graham, "Hollywood: Kelly on Track to Stardom," *Dallas Morning News*, March 21, 1954; **p. 15** "Gentlemen prefer ladies": *Time*, January 31, 1955; **p. 15** "I don't think I'm": Lowry (AP), "These Women," *Van Wert* (Ohio) *Times Bulletin*, December 10, 1954; **p. 15** "Miss Kelly, in the course": "People Are Talking About," *Vogue*, March 1, 1955, p. 130; **p. 15** "unshow-businesslike quality": McCarthy, "The Genteel Miss Kelly," p. 27; **p. 15** "The Girl in White Gloves": "The Girl in White Gloves," *Time*, January 31, 1955, p. 46; **p. 15** Emily Post decreed: Emily Post, *Etiquette: The Blue Book of Social Usage*, rev. ed. (New York: Funk and Wagnalls, 1951), p. 464; **p. 15** "Nobody came": "The Girl in White Gloves," *Time*, January 31, 1955, p. 46; **p. 15** had to diet: Bob Thomas (AP), "Inside Hollywood," *Newport Daily News*, November 1, 1955; **p. 15** smallest size sold: See the Bonwit Teller advertisement for Ben Zuckerman, *Philadelphia Inquirer*, February 15, 1956; **p. 15** Edith Head once listed: Head and Calistro, *Edith Head's Hollywood*, p. 154; **p. 17** "even in a skirt": Erskine Johnson (NEA), "Fame Was Grace's Goal; She Reached It Fast," *Ames* (Iowa) *Daily Tribune*, November 12, 1954; **p. 17** in front of a mirror: Erskine Johnson (NEA), *Indiana* (Pa.) *Evening Gazette*, October 8, 1955. The other four that Helen Rose named were Marlene Dietrich, Claudette Colbert, Jeanmarie, and Audrey Hepburn; **p. 17** "She has a great eye": "Silk and Lace Details Are Released by M-G-M Studio," unidentified Los Angeles newspaper, April 18, 1956; courtesy of the Margaret Herrick Library, Academy of Motion Picture Arts and Sciences, Beverly Hills, California; **p. 17** Eleanor Lambert: See Amy Fine Collins, "The Lady, the List, the Legacy," *Vanity Fair*, April 2004, p. 274; **p. 17** Grace Kelly's debut: Thirteen women were named since there were several ties that year. The alphabetical listing started in 1959 when members of the committee found themselves unable to award ranked honors; **p. 17** "Ten Best-Tailored": "America's Ten Best Tailored Women," *Daily Courier* (Connellsville, Pa.), April 7, 1955; **p. 17** "her personal taste": Associated Press photo caption, September 5, 1955, courtesy of Temple University Urban Archives, Philadelphia; **p. 17** "Ever since she": Emily Belser (UP), "Today's Fashion High Light," *Daily Courier* (Connellsville, Pa.), November 25, 1955. The standards used in making the selection included "ability to select suits which best bring out beauty and figure highlights and personality, skill in 'accessorizing' and choosing correct and interesting color combinations, and the intangible ability to 'wear suits well'" ("'Best-Tailored' Women Are Picked by Experts," *Philadelphia Inquirer*, April 4, 1955); **p. 18** the Grace Kelly Look: "Express the Grace Kelly Look," *Women's Wear Daily*, December 8, 1955; **p. 18** article noted . . . "prominence.": Ibid.; **p. 18** Sculptor Kay Sullivan . . . Mary Brosnan Studios: Judy Jennings, "Grace 'Look' in Windows," *Philadelphia Inquirer*, January 27, 1956; **p. 18** leading American designer: Leonard S. Marcus, *The American Store Window* (New York: Whitney Library of Design, 1978), p. 45; **p. 18** "tops in entertainment": International News Service, "Princess Margaret Woman of the Year," *Newport Daily News*, December 24, 1955; **p. 18** "So great has been": Ibid.; **p. 19** best-tailored women: International News Service, "Grace Kelly Tops List of Ten Best Tailored Women," *Mt. Pleasant* (Iowa) *News*, December 29, 1955; **p. 19** "an almost unprecedented": Olga Curtis (INS), "Grace Kelly Ties for First Place Among World's Best Dressed Women," *Mansfield* (Ohio) *News Journal*, January 5, 1956. The press called attention to the "youth movement," which broke with the traditional recognition of older women— nine of the fourteen names on the 1955 list were under thirty-five years of age, including Princess Margaret Rose of England, born a year after Grace Kelly; **p. 19** Mainbocher: Dorothy Roe (AP), "Grace Kelly, Mrs. Wm. Paley Best Dressed," *Newport Daily News*, January 5, 1956. Mrs. Paley, a former fashion editor, was first married to a member of the Standard Oil family and then to the head of CBS; the tall brunette was almost always at or near the top of the list from 1940 until 1957, when she was elected to the first Fashion Hall of Fame; **p. 19** those who appeared: In the early years of the Best-Dressed List, women professionally connected to fashion were disqualified; starting in 1947 an additional listing of "Best-Dressed Fashion Professionals" allowed for the recognition of industry insiders; **p. 19** "I just buy clothes. . . . my wardrobe contains": "Miss Kelly Talks About Her Clothes," *Evening Bulletin* (Philadelphia), January 5, 1956; **p. 19** "prefer simple clothes": Curtis, "Grace Kelly Ties," *Mansfield* (Ohio) *News Journal*, January 5, 1956; Eleanor Pollock, "Grace Kelly Voted as Best-Dressed," *Evening Bulletin* (Philadelphia), January 5, 1956; **p. 19** "In choosing Miss Kelly": Edrie van Dore, "Grace Kelly Tops Best Dressed List," *Philadelphia Inquirer*, January 5, 1956; **p. 20** "that only the television": Milton Bracker, "Prince of Monaco to Wed Grace Kelly," *New York Times*, January 6, 1956; **p. 20** Hollywood was flabbergasted: Associated Press, "Hollywood Flabbergasted as Grace, Prince Say They'll Wed After Easter," *Newport Daily News*, January 6, 1956; **p. 20** "the biggest bombshell": Associated Press, "Kelly Betrothal Stuns, Pleases Movie Capital," *Philadelphia Inquirer*, January 6, 1956; **p. 20** "queen of . . . prince": "Grace Kelly Will Marry Prince of Monaco in April," *Philadelphia Inquirer*, January 6, 1956; **p. 20** "His Highness's Name": "His Highness' [*sic*] Name Is Pronounced Raynyay," *Evening Bulletin* (Philadelphia), January 5, 1956; **p. 21** "athletically built": Frank H. Weir, "Prince Bejewelled with Titles but He Calls Himself Shorty," *Philadelphia Inquirer*, January 11, 1956. (Oddly, his height is incorrectly given as 5 feet 10 inches.); **p. 21** Grimaldi family: see Françoise de Bernardy, *Princes of Monaco: The Remarkable History of the Grimaldi Family* (London: Arthur Barker, 1961); **p. 21** twenty-five hundred: Reuters, "Grace and Rainier Reunited in Monaco," *Boston Daily Globe*, April 13, 1956; **p. 21** "dreaded taffeta dress": Judith Balaban Quine, *The Bridesmaids: Grace Kelly, Princess of Monaco, and Six Intimate Friends* (New York: Weidenfeld and Nicolson, 1989), p. 107; **p. 21** "most publicized dress": Cynthia Cabot, "Kelly Dress for All," *Philadelphia Inquirer*, January 19, 1956; **p. 22** any girl wishing: Ibid.; **p. 22** "a complete daytime": Helen Rose, *The Glamorous World of Helen Rose* (Palm Springs, Calif.: Helen Rose, 1983), p. 58; **p. 22** ceremony would take place: "Grace Kelly Will Marry Prince of Monaco in April," *Philadelphia Inquirer*, January 6, 1956; **p. 22** Monégasque citizens: Associated Press, "Betrothal Hailed: Monaco Gives Sigh of Relief," *Philadelphia Inquirer*, January 6, 1956; **p. 22** "Roman Catholic weddings": "Grace, Prince Attend New York Society Ball; Monaco Seeks Nuptials," *Philadelphia Inquirer*, January 7, 1956; **p. 22** "There is too much Russia": George Sokolsky, "Too Much Russia," *Marion* (Ohio) *Star*, February 23, 1956; **p. 22** "Almost every American": Elmer Roessner, "No Tie-Ins Allowed," *Chronicle-Telegram* (Elyria, Ohio), March 26, 1956; **p. 24** notice in: *Women's Wear Daily*, March 7, 1956; **p. 24** Max Factor: United Press, "Grace Kelly in Hectic Swirl of Wedding Preparations," *Philadelphia Inquirer*, March 16, 1956; **p. 24** Willys de Mond: Associated Press, "Romantic Interludes: Grace Refuses Stockings," *Boston Daily Globe*, March 27, 1956; he also disclosed the measurements of her ankle, calf, and thigh. See also Harold Heffernan, "Jeweled Nylons Woven for Grace Kelly's Wear," *Evening Bulletin* (Philadelphia), March 2, 1956; **p. 24** After Six Company: Elizabeth Beinkopf, "Grace's Trousseau Top Secret—Not So for Wedding Usher," *Boston Daily Globe*, March 9, 1956; **p. 24** "The prince and I": United Press, "Grace Kelly to Attend Bridesmaid's Wedding, Then Shop for Trousseau," *Coshocton* (Ohio) *Tribune*, March 23, 1956; **p. 24** joked about a cruise: "Horace Sutton's Travels: Monaco Plans a Wedding," *Boston Daily Globe*, April 1, 1956; **p. 24** "in recent weeks": "Grace Kelly Sails in Beige Suit," *Women's Wear Daily*, April 5, 1956; **p. 25** "currently making. . . . pretty this spring": Betty Parkinson, "'Grace Kelly Look' for Spring," *Sunday Bulletin* (Philadelphia), January 15, 1956; **p. 25** "clean-cut kind": Ibid.; **p. 25** clever hairdressers: Arlene C. La Rue, "It's the Grace Kelly Look in Makeup and Hairdos for Spring," *Syracuse* (N.Y.) *Herald-Journal*, February 14, 1956; **pp. 25–27** two completely different feelings. . . . "'pretty—or smart'": Kittie Campbell, "The Grace Kelly Look; The T-Square Silhouette," *Sunday Bulletin* (Philadelphia), February 26, 1956; **p. 27** "Philadelphia's long-stemmed": Kittie Campbell (AP), "Playclothes from French Riviera Reflect Grace Kelly Influence," *Evening Bulletin* (Philadelphia), February 7, 1956; **p. 27** fashion in France: Nadeane Walker (AP), "Ladylike Look Has Influence of Paris Styles," *Newport Daily News*, March 3, 1956; **p. 27** "Apparently la belle Kelly": Campbell, "Playclothes from French Riviera," *Evening Bulletin* (Philadelphia), February 7, 1956; **p. 27** "We hear Kelly": La Rue, "It's the Grace Kelly Look," *Syracuse* (N.Y.) *Herald-Journal*, February 14, 1956; **p. 27** Fashion Academy: United Press, "Mamie, Grace, Margaret Top Best-Dressed," *Berkshire Eagle* (Pittsfield, Mass.), March 27, 1956; **p. 27** "she brings a fragile": Associated Press, "Flowered Hats for Easter," *Newport Daily News*, March 29, 1956; **p. 27** eyeglasses: "Glasses Now Add Glamour," *Philadelphia Inquirer*, March 6, 1956; **p. 27** "Today the ideal": United Press, "Grace Kelly is Influencing Beach Wear," *Monessan* (Pa.) *Daily Independent*, March 22, 1956; **p. 27** "come to be": Blanche Krause, "Tsk, Tsk, Grace—Doesn't Side-Saddle Call for a Skirt?" *Sunday Bulletin* (Philadelphia), April 1, 1956; **p. 27** The trousseau. . . . well-to-do bride: Amy Vanderbilt, *Amy Vanderbilt's Complete Book of Etiquette: A Guide to Gracious Living* (Garden City, N.Y.: Doubleday, 1954), p. 93; **p. 27** household goods: Margaret Bentley, *Wedding Etiquette Complete* (Philadelphia: The John C. Winston Co., 1947), pp. 30–36; **p. 27** monogrammed: "Kellys Mix Up Monogram," *Boston Daily Globe*, March 27, 1956; **p. 27** wardrobe needs at Neiman-Marcus: See Stanley Marcus, *Minding the Store: A Memoir* (Boston: Little, Brown, 1974), p. 191; **p. 27** "Grace is our girl": Kittie Campbell, "Dear Grace Kelly: Don't Pass Us By," *Evening Bulletin* (Philadelphia), February 14, 1956; **p. 28** "I'm so far behind": Associated Press, "Grace Defers Sailing for Europe," *Gettysburg* (Pa.) *Times*, March 8, 1956; **p. 28** a lingerie shower: "Year's Busiest Bride in Whirl of Parties," *Chronicle-Telegram* (Elyria, Ohio), March 29, 1956; **p. 28** shower curtain: United Press, "Grace Kelly Given Shower," *Traverse City* (Mich.) *Record-Eagle*, March 29, 1956. **p. 29** "year's busiest bride": "Year's Busiest Bride," *Chronicle-Telegram* (Elyria, Ohio), March 29, 1956; **p. 29** bride's wedding preparations: "And Now Here Comes The Bride," *Life*, April 9, 1956, pp. 45, 50; **p. 29** sent box . . . finish the orders: Cynthia Cabot, "Grace's Luxurious Trousseau Shows Good Taste," *Philadelphia Inquirer*, April 17, 1956; Kittie Campbell, "Grace Goes All-American in Wedding Wardrobe," *Evening Bulletin* (Philadelphia), April 17, 1956; **p. 29** "Of course, it's easy to dress her": Isabel Johns, "Grace Fully Equipped for Life of Princess," *Boston Daily Globe*, April 18, 1956; **p. 29** presented the requested items: "And the Trousseau," *Women's Wear Daily*, April 5, 1956; **p. 30** also ordered clothes: "Grace Kelly Sails In Beige Suit," *Women's Wear Daily*, April 5, 1956; Cabot, "Grace's Luxurious Trousseau," *Philadelphia Inquirer*, April 17, 1956; **p. 30** "The list of designers": Kittie Campbell, "S.S. Constitution Will Be Floating Fashion Parade," *Evening Bulletin* (Philadelphia), April 4, 1956; **p. 30** Ben Zuckerman . . . collection: "Fashionettes," *Lincoln* (Nebr.) *Sunday Journal and Star*, June 3, 1956; **p. 30** Among the designers: "Blue, Beige Dominate Grace Kelly's Trousseau," *Syracuse* (N.Y.) *Post-Standard*, April 11, 1956; "Grace Kelly's Trousseau Is Based on Blue, Beige," *Berkshire Eagle* (Pittsfield, Mass.), April 6, 1956; "Silk Trousseau for Grace," *Lima* (Ohio) *News*, April 4, 1956; **p. 30** "oodles of short[s]": Johns, "Grace Fully Equipped," *Boston Daily Globe*, April 18, 1956; **p. 30** forty outfits. . . . white to amber: Cabot, "Grace's Luxurious Trousseau," *Philadelphia Inquirer*, April 17, 1956; **p. 30** "French Bread" and "Flax": Campbell, " S.S. Constitution," *Evening Bulletin* (Philadelphia), April 4, 1956; **p. 30** "thrift, discrimination": Campbell, "Grace Goes All-American," *Evening Bulletin* (Philadelphia), April 17, 1956; **p. 30** pairs of shoes: "And Now Here Comes The Bride," p. 50; **p. 30** "gone hat-happy": United Press, "Grace Crams Baggage," *Philadelphia Inquirer*, April 4, 1956; **p. 30** milliners: "Beige, Blue Dominate," *Syracuse* (N.Y.) *Post-Standard*, April 11, 1956; "Grace Kelly's Trousseau," *Berkshire Eagle* (Pittsfield, Mass.), April 6, 1956; "Silk Trousseau," *Lima* (Ohio) *News*, April 4, 1956; Arlene C. La Rue, "Follow This Rule If You Would Pick a Flattering Hat," *Syracuse* (N.Y.) *Herald-Journal*, May 4, 1956; **p. 30** Mr. Fred of John Fredericks: A number of newspapers featured a photo of the designer fitting his famous client in a trousseau chapeau. See, for example, "Bonnet for The Trousseau," *Zanesville* (Ohio) *Signal*, February 25, 1956; Blanche Krause, "Mr. Fred Designs for Grace Kelly," *Evening Bulletin* (Philadelphia), March 6, 1956; **p. 30** Sally Victor: "Even the Prince 'Buys American,' for Grace Kelly," *Evening Bulletin* (Philadelphia), April 4, 1956; **p. 30** straw hat: "15 Police and 3 Detectives Guard Grace at Easter Mass," *Philadelphia Inquirer*, April 2, 1956; **p. 30** "a powerful stimulation. . . . equal to any in the world": Cabot, "Grace's Luxurious Trousseau," *Philadelphia Inquirer*, April 17, 1956; **p. 31** "When it was announced": Chierichetti, *Edith Head*, pp. 129–30. See also Head and Calistro, *Edith Head's Hollywood*, pp. 113–14; **p. 31** giving their stars wedding gowns: Rose, *The Glamorous World of Helen Rose*, p. 27; **p. 32** Helen Rose had designed: International News Service, "Helen Rose Asked to Create Grace Kelly's Wedding Gown,"

Syracuse (N.Y.) *Herald-Journal*, January 25, 1956. Here Helen Rose also stated that she "warns" stars that she won't design more than two wedding gowns for them. "I tell them they'd better hold on to the second husband because if they don't they'll never get another wedding dress from me!" The designer added, however, that she didn't think it was necessary to hand out this type of advice to Grace Kelly, "'I thing [*sic*] this marriage is for keeps,' she said. 'Grace is the kind of girl who makes up her mind and sticks to it.'"; **p. 32** MGM . . . continued to pay: Englund, *Grace of Monaco*, p. 149; **p. 32** "During the shooting": Rose, *Just Make Them Beautiful*, p. 105. By 1983, Helen Rose remembered the situation differently: "When Grace announced her forthcoming marriage and the studio asked what she wanted for a wedding gift, she told them, 'I would like my two wedding outfits to be made at MGM and designed by Helen Rose'" (Rose, *The Glamorous World of Helen Rose*, p. 28); **p. 33** Adrian: Adrian's full name was Adrian Adolph Greenburg; **p. 33** Irene: Irene's full name was Irene Lentz Gibbons; **p. 33** Academy Awards: Separate costume design awards were given for black-and-white and color films through 1966; **p. 33** visual allure: David Chierichetti, *Hollywood Costume Design* (New York: Harmony Books, 1976), pp. 40–41; **p. 33** She designed: Helen Rose had also already designed the costumes for what was to be Grace Kelly's next film, *Designing Women*, which was to begin filming in June 1956; based on an idea from the designer, it was a glossy version of her life and "a clothes film." It was filmed with Lauren Bacall in the role Grace Kelly was to have played.; **p. 33** several conferences: "Silk and Lace Details Are Released by M-G-M Studio," unidentified Los Angeles newspaper, April 18, 1956; courtesy of the Margaret Herrick Library, Academy of Motion Picture Arts and Sciences, Beverly Hills, California; **p. 33** a long train: Ibid.; **p. 33** "I explained to": Rose, *Just Make Them Beautiful*, p. 105; **p. 33** "She is a dream": "Silk and Lace Details Are Released by M-G-M Studio," unidentified Los Angeles newspaper, April 18, 1956; courtesy of the Margaret Herrick Library, Academy of Motion Picture Arts and Sciences, Beverly Hills, California; **p. 33** "upset style": "Dorothy McGuire Bridal Gown Ignores Tradition," *The Newark* (Ohio) *Advocate and American Tribune*, March 15, 1952; **p. 33** "welded together" . . . supposed advantage: Ibid.; **p. 33** "the largest and": "Silk and Lace Details Are Released by M-G-M Studio," unidentified Los Angeles newspaper, April 18, 1956; courtesy of the Margaret Herrick Library, Academy of Motion Picture Arts and Sciences, Beverly Hills, California; **p. 33** "designs and": Profile of the wardrobe department in the studio's employee newsletter, "Know Your Studio," *Inside MGM*, September 21, 1951, courtesy of the Margaret Herrick Library, Academy of Motion Picture Arts and Sciences, Beverly Hills, California; **p. 33** embroidery department: Rose, *Just Make Them Beautiful*, p. 64; **p. 33** "When I told her": Fay Hammond, "Grace's Bridal Gown Has Veil—of Secrecy," *Los Angeles Times*, April 10, 1956; **p. 34** "Every manufacturer. . . . its construction": Mal Caplan quoted in Rose, *Just Make Them Beautiful*, p. 107; **p. 34** "fancy fitting rooms. . . . concerned": Aline Mosby, "Grace Kelly's Wedding Dress to be 'Simple but Elegant,'" *Evening Bulletin* (Philadelphia), February 4, 1956; **p. 34** "a bridal veil": Louella Parsons, "Grace Sails on April 4," *Philadelphia Inquirer*, February 15, 1956; **p. 34** "as closely guarded": Cynthia Lowry, "Wedding Plans of Grace, Margaret," *Boston Sunday Globe*, March 25, 1956; **p. 34** "currently the most": Katherine Vincent, "Designer Buttons Lip on Grace's Gown," *Philadelphia Daily News*, April 11, 1956; **p. 34** Miss Kelly herself: Bob Thomas, "Grace Announced Wedding Schedule," *Philadelphia Inquirer*, February 25, 1956; **p. 34** "I'm surprised that": Edrie van Dore, "That Bridal Gown Is Still a Secret," *Philadelphia Inquirer*, April 11, 1956; **p. 34** previous bridal design: Mosby, "Grace Kelly's Wedding Dress," *Evening Bulletin* (Philadelphia), February 4, 1956; Elizabeth Harrison, "Designer Mum on Kelly Dress," *New York Times*, March 20, 1956; **p. 34** "reporting breathlessly": "Year's Busiest Bride," *Chronicle-Telegram* (Elyria, Ohio), March 29, 1956; **p. 34** "the Big Question. . . . waist up!": Evelyn Hayes, "Grace's Designer Keeps Mum," *Washington Post*, April 12, 1956; **p. 34** "reliable sources": "Crisp Silks and Laces for Grace's Wedding Dresses," *Women's Wear Daily*, April 5, 1956; **p. 34** *Motion Picture*, caption of the sketch, April 16, 1956, courtesy of Top Foto; **p. 34** strongly repudiated: "Kelly Wedding: Helen Rose Calls Unpublished Sketches Unauthentic," *Women's Wear Daily*, April 9, 1956; **p. 34** "Because she is a kind": Cynthia Cabot, "Bride's Garb Expected to Set Trend," *Philadelphia Inquirer*, April 15, 1956; **p. 35** "First specific word": "White Satin Wedding Shoes for Grace Kelly," *Evening Bulletin* (Philadelphia), February 27, 1956; **p. 35** David Evins, born: Obituary for David Evins, *New York Times*, December 29, 1991; **p. 36** tore when stretched: Marilyn Evins, interview by the author, August 23, 2005; **p. 36** "David Evins is making": Walter Winchell, "On Broadway," *Mansfield* (Ohio) *News Journal*, March 1, 1956; **p. 36** the idea that Miss Kelly wore flats: See, for example, Colin McDowell, *Shoes: Fashion and Fantasy* (New York: Rizzoli, 1989), p. 193; **p. 36** "with an appreciation": "White Satin Wedding Shoes for Grace Kelly," *Evening Bulletin* (Philadelphia), February 27, 1956; **p. 36** "must at least pay": Post, *Etiquette*, p. 251; **p. 36** Devout mid-twentieth-century brides: Bentley, *Wedding Etiquette Complete*, p. 246; **pp. 36–37** gift from long-time friend: Ruth Seltzer, "The Philadelphia Scene," *Evening Bulletin* (Philadelphia), April 10, 1956; **p. 37** In her book. . . . "delicate flowers": Rose, *Just Make Them Beautiful*, p. 106; **p. 37** Miss Rose says: Ibid., p. 107; **p. 37** Gant Gaither: Gant Gaither, *Princess of Monaco: The Story of Grace Kelly* (New York: Henry Holt, 1957), p. 94; **p. 37** Miss Rose reported: Rose, *Just Make Them Beautiful*, p. 107; **p. 37** detailed pressing instructions: Hammond, "Grace's Bridal Gown," *Los Angeles Times*, April 10, 1956; **p. 38** names of her bridal attendants: "Eight Bridesmaids to Attend Grace," *Philadelphia Inquirer*, February 22, 1956. Princess Antoinette was also named as an attendant, and a dress was made for her. J. Randy Taraborrelli, who had access to an unpublished manuscript about Princess Antoinette, says she was offended at being treated like one of the bride's girlfriends and did not wear the clothes brought from the United States. (See J. Randy Taraborrelli, *Once Upon a Time: Behind the Fairy Tale of Princess Grace and Prince Rainier* [New York: Warner Books, 2003], p. 167); **p. 39** sending vice president: International News Service photo caption, March 25, 1956, courtesy of Corbis; **p. 39** "a great coup": Marcus, *Minding the Store*, p. 191; **p. 39** Joseph Allen Hong: Obituary for Joseph Allen Hong, *San Francisco Chronicle*, March 29, 2004, and Jeanie Beenk, Hong's sister, telephone interview by the author, June 6, 2005; **p. 40** "first big job": Photo caption, *Chronicle-Telegram* (Elyria, Ohio), March 29, 1956; **p. 40** "close guess": Olga Curtis (INS), "Fantasy Effect, Back Interest Due in Gowns of Grace's Bridesmaids," *Lima* (Ohio) *News*, March 20, 1956; "Grace's Attendants Get Jewel Colors," *Syracuse* (N.Y.) *Herald-Journal*, March 21, 1956, and "Preview of Kelly Gowns," *Philadelphia Inquirer*, March 21, 1956; **p. 40** "back interest," denied by: "Store Denies Kelly Bridesmaids Gown Descriptions," *Women's Wear Daily*, March 21, 1956; **p. 40** released descriptions: International News Service photo caption, March 26, 1956, courtesy of Corbis; photo caption, *Chronicle-Telegram* (Elyria, Ohio), March 29, 1956; **p. 40** Monaco event: Frances Burns, "Fast Work Gets Kelly Bridesmaids' Dresses—Daffodil Yellow—Aboard Ship in Time," *Evening Bulletin* (Philadelphia), April 3, 1956; **p. 40** "marked by the": International News Service photo caption, March 26, 1956, courtesy of Corbis; **p. 40** favorite color: Helen Rose quoted in Hammond, "Grace's Bridal Gown," *Los Angeles Times*, April 10, 1956; **p. 40** "Sunlight": International News Service photo caption, March 26, 1956, courtesy of Corbis; **p. 40** contrast to the grayness: International News Service, "'Preview' of Kelly Gowns," *Philadelphia Inquirer*, March 21, 1956; **p. 40** prestigious commission: Since so many people and companies were involved, credit for the design of the bridesmaids' dresses is confusing—and it was even at the time, as a perplexed reader's letter to the Philadelphia *Evening Bulletin* on April 9, 1956, makes clear. While both Neiman-Marcus and Priscilla of Boston were involved, Joe Hong's design work has not been remembered, and Mrs. Kidder is often cited as the designer of the attendants' dresses (and sometimes even credited with designing Grace Kelly's wedding dress). In addition, Helen Rose later claimed that she (or "we" at the studio) had designed the bridesmaids' dresses as well as the wedding dress. See Rose, *Just Make Them Beautiful*, pp. 105–6, and a letter from Helen Rose to Mrs. Kidder, May 29, 1981, in the Priscilla of Boston Collection at the National Museum of American History Archives. I thank Kay Peterson for bringing this letter to my attention; **p. 40** Priscilla Comins Kidder: Frances Burns, "Hub Shop Puts Last Stitch in Gowns for Grace's Party," *Boston Sunday Globe*, April 1, 1956; Rosemary Feitelberg, "Remembering Priscilla Kidder," *Women's Wear Daily*, December 23, 2003; **p. 40** slight modifications: International News Service photo caption, March 26, 1956, courtesy of Corbis. In the Philadelphia *Evening Bulletin* of April 3, 1956, Mrs. Kidder said she was sent a sketch of the gowns that she modified; she also stated that she selected the exact shade of the specified color—"a soft, warm, sunny, color"—and the fabrics; **p. 40** "Custom sewing": Burns, "Hub Shop," *Boston Sunday Globe*, April 1, 1956; **p. 41** "excited, enthusiastic": Frances Burns, "Fast Work," *Evening Bulletin* (Philadelphia), April 3, 1956; **p. 41** Kidders drove: "Hub Shop," *Boston Sunday Globe*, April 1, 1956; **p. 41** "micrometric". . . fit the dress: "Grace's Attendant Told Not to Gain Weight," *Newport Daily News*, April 3, 1956. Bettina Gray lamented that she therefore would not be able to indulge in the rich food and wine aboard ship. Reflecting the dieting strategy of many American women at the time, she said sadly, "It looks like a cottage cheese and steak trip." George Croft, "Grays Leave Today for Monaco Wedding," *Boston Daily Globe*, April 3, 1956; **p. 41** Greek shepherds: Photo caption, *Chronicle-Telegram* (Elyria, Ohio), March 29, 1956; **p. 41** misty hairbraid . . . butterfly bow: International News Service photo caption, March 26, 1956, courtesy of Corbis. "Butterfly bow" was misquoted in several articles to read "a small butterfly at the back"; see, for example, the photo caption in the *Chronicle-Telegram* (Elyria, Ohio), March 29, 1956; **p. 41** milliner Don Marshall: Quine, *Bridesmaids*, pp. 144, 407; *Dictionnaire de la mode au XXe siècle*, ed. Bruno Remaury (Paris: Éditions du Regard, 1994), p. 175; **p. 41** Don Marshall appeared: Obituary for Don Marshall, *New York Times*, May 11, 1995; Quine, *Bridesmaids*, pp. 144, 407; *Dictionnaire de la mode*, p. 175; **p. 42** tiered hats: The Museum was given three yellow broad-brimmed hats by Mrs. John B. Kelly in 1963, when the matron of honor's dress was given. Two of the hats are made of organza, and one of them was identified at the time as going with the matron of honor dress; another identical organza hat, while not identified at the time, is probably the matron of honor hat made for Princess Antoinette and not used in the wedding. A third hat, also not identified, is of horsehair, the style worn by the six bridesmaids. It is not known to which bridesmaid the hat belonged, although it is not that of Maree Frisby Pamp Rambo, since she had hers into the 1990s before it was misplaced; **p. 42** the Kellys paid: Quine, *Bridesmaids*, p. 144; **p. 42** Mary Carter of Dallas: "Priscilla May Gown Kelly Bridesmaids," *Women's Wear Daily*, March 8, 1956; "Priscilla Confirms Execution of Kelly Bridesmaids' Gowns," *Women's Wear Daily*, March 27, 1956; Ruth Holman Baker, "Dallas-Made Fashions To Parade for Press," *Dallas Morning News*, March 18, 1956; "Mary Carter Adds New Fashion Honor," *Dallas Morning News*, August 17, 1958. I thank Bryan McKinney at the Dallas Public Library for his help with this information; **p. 42** miniature daisies: According to *Women's Wear Daily*, these were made by milliner Therse (Therese) Ahrens. "Daisy Halos for Wedding Attendants," *Women's Wear Daily*, April 20, 1956; **p. 42** "thrifty Aunt Grace": Quine, *Bridesmaids*, p. 198; **p. 42** standard for ring bearers: Post, *Etiquette*, p. 210; **p. 42** "accompanied by": Associated Press, "Grace Kelly Leaves Today for Wedding," *Gettysburg* (Pa.) *Times*, April 5, 1956; **p. 42** "cool as a cucumber": United Press, "Weeping Grace Sails for Monaco and Life as Royal Princess," *Philadelphia Inquirer*, April 5, 1956; **p. 42** "the story feminine": "Grace Kelly Sails Today," *Boston Daily Globe*, April 4, 1956; **p. 42** "four trunks and": Associated Press, "Grace Kelly Sails to Marry Prince as Crowd Jams Pier for Sendoff," *Syracuse* (N.Y.) *Post-Standard*, April 5, 1956; **p. 42** not ready: Cynthia Cabot, "Grace's Luxurious Trousseau," *Philadelphia Inquirer*, April 17, 1956; **p. 42** favorite old clothes: Gaither, *Princess of Monaco*, p. 74; **p. 42** "All the passengers": "'Don't Let Protocol Get You,' John B. Advises Bride-to-Be," *Evening Bulletin* (Philadelphia), April 9, 1956; **p. 42** "Pale Princess": United Press, "Grace Previews 'Pale Princess Look' at Sea," *Evening Bulletin* (Philadelphia), April 6, 1956; **p. 42** "floating fashion parade": Kittie Campbell, "S.S. Constitution," *Evening Bulletin* (Philadelphia), April 4, 1956; **p. 43** "I'm sure we're": Isabel Johns, "Grace Fully Equipped," *Boston Daily Globe*, April 18, 1956; **p. 43** different evening dress: Cabot, "Bride's Garb," *Philadelphia Inquirer*, April 15, 1956; **p. 43** mother of the bride: Cynthia Cabot, "Mrs. Kelly Selects Costumes," *Philadelphia Inquirer*, March 28, 1956; **p. 43** "long stories": "Cabot, "Bride's Garb," *Philadelphia Inquirer*, April 15, 1956; **p. 43** Hazel Markel: Evelyn Hayes, "Here's Wardrobe for The Wedding," *Washington Post*, April 7, 1956; **p. 43** "certainly the first": Cabot, "Bride's Garb," *Philadelphia Inquirer*, April 15, 1956; **p. 43** "scrubbed": Paul Ghali, "Monaco Scrubbed Like New Baby," *Boston Daily Globe*, March 20, 1956; **p. 43** fifty thousand: Bob Considine, "Grace and Her Prince Steal a Few Moments After Happiest of Days," *Philadelphia Inquirer*, April 13, 1956; **p. 43** worried about: Bob Considine (INS), "Grace Arrives at Cannes to Meet Prince," *Philadelphia Inquirer*, April 12, 1956. Prince Rainier also worried about what to wear for this momentous reunion, deciding at the last minute to substitute a dark blue suit for the admiral's uniform he had planned to wear. Elizabeth Toomey, "Grace Reunited with Rainier," *Evening Bulletin* (Philadelphia), April 12, 1956; **p. 43** navy: Olga Curtis (INS), "Fancy, Big Hats; High-Waisted Empire Silhouettes to Lead in Sunday Parade," *Lima* (Ohio) *News*, March 30, 1956; **p. 43** coat featured: Quine also relates that when she found herself wearing an identical Zuckerman coat for the disembarkation, she quickly took it off and furtively stashed it behind a funnel vent. Quine, *Bridesmaids*, pp. 27–28. See also "Fashionettes," *Lincoln* (Nebr.) *Sunday Journal and Star*, June 3, 1956; **p. 44** "The only females": Curtis, "Fancy, Big Hats," *Lima* (Ohio) *News*, March 30, 1956; **p. 44** "Kelly trademark . . . to wear": Ibid.; **p. 44** "as big as": Bob Considine (INS), "Flowers Rain Like Confetti as Grace Arrives in Monaco," *Independent* (Pasadena, Calif.), April 13, 1956; **p. 44** "her flying saucer . . . off the deck": Bob Considine (INS), "Monaco Embraces Grace in Joyous Celebration," *Syracuse* (N.Y.) *Herald-Journal*, April 12, 1956; **p. 44** orchid lei: Considine, "Grace and Her Prince," *Philadelphia Inquirer*, April 13, 1956; **p. 44** Ann Valde: Considine, "Flowers Rain," *Independent* (Pasadena, Calif.), April 13, 1956; **p. 44** "I have heard": Associated Press, "Grace-ful Bits," *Boston Daily Globe*, April 16, 1956; **p. 45** "a simple wedding": Art Buchwald, "P.S. From Texas," *Newport Daily News*, March 30, 1956; **p. 45** "There won't be". . . . photographers: "They'll Write at Grace's Wedding," *Boston Daily Globe*, April 4, 1956; **p. 45** "Are you interested. . . . *Post Standard*?": "P-S Wedding Coverage Will Be 'The Greatest,'" *Syracuse* (N.Y.) *Post-Standard*, April 8, 1956; **p. 45** *TV Guide*: Advertisement in *Philadelphia Inquirer*, April 11, 1956; **p. 45** "I believe this": Eddy Gilmore, "Press at Wedding Will Have Serpentine Bar, Own Chapel," *Evening Bulletin* (Philadelphia), April 5, 1956; **p. 45** 1,800 had been: United Press, "Wedding Newsier Than Summit Talks," *Boston Daily Globe*, April 16, 1956; **p. 45** "the distinct impression. . . . everyday life": John Crosby, "This Year of Grace," *Independent* (Pasadena, Calif.), April 16, 1956; **p. 45** "sad commentary": Mrs. Edward R. Murrow quoted in Janet Steinfeld, "Lecturer Discusses 'Fear' Role," *Barnard Bulletin* (New York: Barnard College), April 23, 1956; **p. 45** letter printed: Grace M. Barber, letter to the editor, *Boston Daily Globe*, April 25, 1956; **p. 45** "I want the richest": North American Newspaper Alliance, "Kelly-Rainier Rites to Dazzle Riviera," *Marion* (Ohio) *Star*, February 2, 1956; **p. 45** One couple was: Cynthia Lowry (AP), "Monaco Wedding Guests to Need 23 Different Costumes," *Lima* (Ohio) *News*, March 30, 1956; **p. 45** "starry-eyed": Peg Simpson, "Grace Kelly Nuptials to Provide Radio, TV with Royal Carnival," *Syracuse* (N.Y.) *Post-Standard*, March 25, 1956; **p. 45** thirty thousand visitors: "Press," *Newsweek*, April 16, 1956, p. 71; **p. 45** "an impressive array": Inez Robb, "Monegasque Doctors Should Prepare for Epidemic among Non-Invitees," *Syracuse* (N.Y.) *Post-Standard*, April 13, 1956; **p. 45** "the clothes horse": Elizabeth Toomey (UP), "Clothes, Jewels, Fill Monaco with Luggage," *Boston Daily Globe*, April 19, 1956; **p. 45** Parisian designers: "Ordered in Paris for Monaco Festivities," *Women's Wear Daily*, April 12, 1956. Europeans had to stipulate that trendy short evening dresses be lengthened for the formal occasions. "Want Long Gowns In Paris for Monaco Wedding," *Women's Wear Daily*, March 21, 1956; **p. 45** Roman fashion houses: "Ordered at Rome Dressmakers For Guests at Monaco," *Women's Wear Daily*, April 16, 1956; **p. 45** U.S. designers: "Ordered in N.Y. for Monaco Festivities," *Women's Wear Daily*, April 3, 1956; "More Fashions Destined for Monaco," *Women's Wear Daily*, April 10, 1956; **p. 45** "Never have so many": Elizabeth Toomey (UP), "Clothes, Jewels," *Boston Daily Globe*, April 19, 1956; **p. 45** Bermuda shorts: Photo caption, *Philadelphia Inquirer*, April 16, 1956; see also Polly Platt, "Grace's Sister Wears Shorts to Lunch with Prince's Kin," *Evening Bulletin* (Philadelphia), April 13, 1956; **p. 46** "what pants to": "Hilton Instructed on Pants to Wear," *Philadelphia Inquirer*, April 18, 1956; **p. 46** W-Day: Alice F. Keegan, "Tully-ites Visited Prince's Palace before Grace," *Syracuse* (N.Y.) *Post-Standard*, April 13, 1956; **p. 46** disparaging names: E. J. Kahn, Jr., "The Wayward Press," *New Yorker*, May 5, 1956, pp. 158–59; Bob Considine (INS), "Grace and Her Prince," *Philadelphia Inquirer*, April 13, 1956; and "Movies' Pretty Princess Assumes a Real Life Title," *Life*, April 30, 1956, p. 36; **p. 46** a new song: Kahn, "The Wayward Press," p. 160; **p. 47** car mobbed: Elizabeth Toomey (UP), "Prince Rainier Bars Photographers from Palace after Hectic Encounter," *Evening Bulletin* (Philadelphia), April 13, 1956; **p. 47** "a picture of fragile": Elizabeth Toomey (UP), "Grace, Prince Rehearse Wedding in Cathedral," *Sheboygan* (Wisc.) *Press*, April 16, 1956; **p. 47** "I'll be glad": Associated Press, "Grace, Prince Plan to Live in Villa 'Ibera,'" *Lima* (Ohio) *News*, April 18, 1956; **p. 47** "All I want": Toomey, "Grace, Prince Rehearse," *Sheboygan* (Wisc.) *Press*, April 16, 1956; **p. 47** "considered the biggest": Henry Giniger, "Rainier and Miss Kelly to Marry in Civil Ceremony Today and Religious Rites Tomorrow—Nuptial Dress Described," *New York Times*, April 18, 1956; **p. 47** "MGM made sure": United Press, "Princess to Walk Down The Aisle in 5-Skirted Lace-Taffeta Dress," *Wisconsin State Journal*, April 18, 1956; **p. 47** "the most lavish": Emily Belser (INS), "400 Yards in Gown for Grace," *Independent* (Pasadena, Calif.), April 18, 1956; **p. 47** "raved the dress": UP, "Princess to Walk Down The Aisle," *Wisconsin State Journal*, April 18, 1956; **p. 47** "because we used": Belser, "400 Yards," *Independent* (Pasadena, Calif.), April 18, 1956; **p. 47** "It frightens me": UP, "Princess to Walk Down The Aisle," *Wisconsin State Journal*, April 18, 1956; most expensive: Rose, *Just Make Them Beautiful*, p. 106; **p. 47** Marusia: Belser, "400 Yards," *Independent* (Pasadena, Calif.), April 18, 1956; **p. 47** $7,266.68: Englund, *Grace of Monaco*, p. 149, repeated, for example, in James Spada, *Grace: The Secret Lives of a Princess* (Garden City, N.Y.: Doubleday, 1987), **p. 47** "When the estimate": Rose, *Just Make Them Beautiful*, p. 107; **p. 47** "full recipe": UP, "Princess to Walk Down Aisle," *Wisconsin State Journal*, April 18, 1956; **p. 47** "400 Yards": Belser, "400 Yards," *Independent* (Pasadena, Calif.), April 18, 1956; **p. 47** "used up to 450 yards": Photo caption, *Life*, May 14, 1956, p. 66; **p. 47** exaggerated estimates: While some, such as Robert Lacey (*Grace* [New York: G. P. Putnam's Sons, 1994], p. 263) and Phyllida Hart-Davies (*Grace: The Story of a Princess* [New York: St. Martin's Press, 1982], p. 80) repeat the amounts of the "full recipe," sometimes the amounts vary slightly: Quine has 98 yards of tulle and 320 of Valenciennes lace (see Quine, *Bridesmaids*, p. 198); Taraborrelli still repeats 450 yards of lace and taffeta in 2005 (see Taraborrelli, *Once Upon a Time*, p. 183); **p. 48** The lace used: For information on nineteenth century rose point (*point de gaze*) lace, see Pat Earnshaw, *A Dictionary of Lace* (Aylesbury, U.K.: Shire Publications, 1982), especially pp. 131, 147–48; Pat Earnshaw, *The Identification of Lace* (Aylesbury, U.K.: Shire Publications, 1980), especially pp. 56–57, 60; Santina Levey, *Lace: A History* (London: Victoria and Albert Museum/W. S. Maney and Son, 1983), especially p. 109; and Patricia Wardle, *Victorian Lace* (London: Herbert Jenkins, 1968), especially pp. 30–31, 128–30. The term rose point was also retroactively applied in the nineteenth century to describe earlier lace; while it could be applied more broadly to all raised needlepoint laces, this term or *point de rose* started to be used to distinguish medium-sized raised Venetian needle lace of the later seventeenth century from the larger scale *gros point* and the smaller scale *point de neige*. See Earnshaw, *Dictionary*, p. 147, and Levey, *Lace*, pp. 32–35; **p. 48** "Rose point is": Marian Powys, *Lace and Lace-Making* (Boston: Charles T. Branford, 1953), p. 140; **p. 48** Valenciennes: For information on Valenciennes

lace, see Earnshaw, *Dictionary*, p. 177; Pat Earnshaw, *How to Recognise Machine Laces* (Guildford: Gorse Publications, 1995), especially pp. 92–93; and Pat Earnshaw, *Lace in Fashion* (London: B. T. Batsford, 1985), especially p. 139; **p. 48** peau de soie . . . gros de Londres: Mary Brooks Picken, *The Fashion Dictionary: Fabric, Sewing, and Dress as Expressed in the Language of Fashion* (New York: Funk and Wagnall's, 1957), p. 246; **p. 51** "gros de longre": Rose, *Just Make Them Beautiful*, p. 106; **p. 51** "in regal style": Associated Press, "Grace Wearing 'Regal Style' Wedding Dress," *Two Rivers* (Wisc.) *Reporter*, April 18, 1956; **p. 51** long-sleeved bodice: Belser, "400 Yards," *Independent* (Pasadena, Calif.), April 18, 1956; **p. 51** "masterpiece of": Associated Press, "Miss Kelly's Gown Is Described as 'Regal,'" *Fort Atkinson* (Wisc.) *Union*, April 18, 1956; Juliet cap: "Wedding Dress of Grace a 'Spectacular,'" *Los Angeles Times*, April 18, 1956; **p. 52** circular veil: Associated Press, "Miss Kelly's Gown," *Fort Atkinson* (Wisc.) *Union*, April 18, 1956; **p. 52** worn separately: Ibid.; Associated Press, "35 Persons Spent 6 Weeks Making Wedding Dress," *Evening Bulletin* (Philadelphia), April 18, 1956. Helen Rose later resketched the wedding dress for her book *The Glamorous World of Helen Rose* (p. 31) to include a back view of the underpinnings as a strapless evening dress with flounced skirt; **p. 52** 3 1/2 yards long: Associated Press, "Grace Wearing," *Two Rivers* (Wisc.) *Reporter*, April 18, 1956; French Museum for $2,500: Rose, *Just Make Them Beautiful*, p. 106; repeated, for example, in Sarah Bradford, *Princess Grace* (New York: Stein and Day, 1984), p. 139, and Jayne Ellen Wayne, *Grace Kelly's Men* (New York: St. Martin's Press, 1991), p. 285; **p. 52** "naturally not so . . . roses taffeta": Emily Belser (INS), "300 Yards of Lace in Grace's Gown," *Philadelphia Inquirer*, April 18, 1956; **p. 52** mistranslated: Photo caption, *Syracuse* (N.Y.) *Post-Standard*, April 18, 1956; **p. 52** "the biggest thing": Robb, "Monegasque Doctors," *Syracuse* (N.Y.) *Post-Standard*, April 13, 1956; **p. 52** warned some: Betty Beale, *Syracuse* (N.Y.) *Herald-American*, March 25, 1956. In 1997, Mrs. Joseph S. Rambo gave the Museum the strapless light brown lace ball gown and petticoat designed by James Galanos that she had worn (as bridesmaid Maree Frisby Pamp) to the opera gala; **p. 52** "The clothes are": Toomey (UP), "Clothes, Jewels," *Boston Daily Globe*, April 19, 1956; **p. 52** from Lanvin: "Grace to Wear Gown by Lanvin," *Syracuse* (N.Y.) *Post-Standard*, March 9, 1956. Both Quine (*Bridesmaids*, p. 160) and Gaither (*Princess of Monaco*, p. 110) say the Lanvin dress was only ordered when the bride arrived in Monaco, but newspaper accounts contradict this; **p. 52** embroidered with: Sketch caption, *Women's Wear Daily*, March 30, 1956; **p. 52** "the Goya manner": specially created: Peggy Massin (Reuters), "'Her Grace' to Wear a Lanvin Gown on First Appearance as Princess," *Evening Bulletin* (Philadelphia), April 9, 1956; **p. 53** "a glittering assemblage": Associated Press, "Oscar Winner, Monaco Prince Wed Amid 'Pomp, Ceremony,'" *Indiana* (Pa.) *Evening Gazette*, April 19, 1956; **p. 53** "Brand new protocol": "Monaco Decrees Blue Garb," *Philadelphia Inquirer*, March 19, 1956; **p. 54** popular midcentury choice: O. E. Schoeffler and William Gale, *Esquire's Encyclopedia of 20th Century Men's Fashions* (New York: McGraw-Hill, 1973), p. 247; Post, *Etiquette*, p. 473; Vanderbilt, *Amy Vanderbilt's Complete Book of Etiquette*, pp. 146, 148; **p. 54** short, covered-up neutral dresses: United Press, "Wedding Attire Is a Puzzle to Philadelphians in Monaco," *Evening Bulletin* (Philadelphia), April 18, 1956; Associated Press, "Prince to Wed in a Uniform Like Napoleon's Aides Wore," *Ironwood* (Mich.) *Daily Globe*, April 6, 1956; **p. 54** suits to evening gowns: Ilka Chase, "Ilka Feels Sorry for Grace on Brilliant Wedding Day," *Syracuse* (N.Y.) *Post-Standard*, April 20, 1956; **p. 54** woolen underwear: "Today . . . in Monaco," *Women's Wear Daily*, April 19, 1956; **p. 54** monotone outfits . . . pastel hues: Judy Jennings, "Pastel Hues Favored by Phila. Guests," *Philadelphia Inquirer*, April 15, 1956; "Fashions at Monaco Wedding: Full Skirted Summery Ensembles, Airy Hats," *Women's Wear Daily*, April 20, 1956; **p. 54** "caught every eye": Polly Platt, "Fashion Show Provided by Philadelphia Guests," *Evening Bulletin* (Philadelphia), April 19, 1956; **p. 54** "were divided as to": Jane Cianfarra, "Fashions of U.S. Star in Monaco," *New York Times*, April 20, 1956; **p. 54** sent instructions: Quine, *Bridesmaids*, p. 198; **p. 54** blue satin bows:

According to Helen Rose, *Just Make Them Beautiful*, p. 106. No evidence of the bows remains; **p. 54** re-embroidered by: "How Grace Kelly's Bridal Gowns Were Constructed: Stitch by Stitch," *Women's Wear Daily*, April 18, 1956; **p. 56** "something borrowed": Gaither, *Princess of Monaco*, p. 79; **p. 57** "Miss Kelly's ascension": Kahn, "The Wayward Press," p. 158; **p. 58** given to them by: United Press, "Rainier Buys Gift Dresses," *Philadelphia Inquirer*, March 16, 1956; **p. 58** going-away outfit: The press does not seem to have mentioned any involvement by Edith Head with Princess Grace's going away outfit at the time; **p. 61** "truly beautiful": "Grace, Prince Sail Away, All Alone on Honeymoon," *Philadelphia Inquirer*, April 20, 1956; **p. 61** "Her manner made": Bob Considine (INS), "Grace and Prince Sail Away on Honeymoon," *Herald-Journal*, April 19, 1956; **p. 61** "Grace was gorgeous": Associated Press, "Grace, Prince Take Church Vows; Nervous Rainier Can't Get Ring On," *Newport Daily News*, April 19, 1956; **p. 61** "like a river": Considine, "Grace and Prince Sail," *Syracuse* (N.Y.) *Herald-Journal*, April 19, 1956; **p. 61** "Her bridal gown was": Ilka Chase, "Ilka Feels Sorry for Grace," *Syracuse* (N.Y.) *Post-Standard*, April 20, 1956; **p. 61** "the loveliest example": Cianfarra, "Fashions of U.S.," *New York Times*, April 20, 1956; **p. 61** film was rushed: Reuters, "Wedding Films Flown to U.S.," *Boston Daily Globe*, April 20, 1956; **p. 61** "only complete coverage": Advertisement in *Oakland* (Calif.) *Tribune*, May 20, 1956; **p. 61** "The Grace Kelly–Prince Rainier": Advertisement in the *Evening Bulletin* (Philadelphia), April 19, 1956; **p. 61** "Monaco Bridal Fever": "New York Catches Monaco Bridal Fever," *Women's Wear Daily*, April 19, 1956; **p. 61** "copied, re-copied. . . . wind-swept trains": Edrie van Dore, "Grace's Gown Is Copied," *Philadelphia Inquirer*, April 20, 1956; **p. 61** "lady-like, covered-up": Dorothy Roe, "Choose a Dream of a Gown for Most Important Day," *St. Joseph's* (Mich.) *Herald-Press*, May 9, 1956; **p. 61** "Grace Kelly crown": "Lt. Marvin Oliver Exchanges Vows with Margaret Schaefer," *Oakland* (Calif.) *Tribune*, September 23, 1956; **p. 61** certain bridal trends: Roe, "Choose a Dream of a Gown," *St. Joseph's* (Mich.) *Herald-Press*, May 9, 1956; **p. 61** "stunning blow. . . . golden opportunity": Bernard Kaplan (NANA), "Paris is Dealt a Blow," *Evening Bulletin* (Philadelphia), May 2, 1956; **p. 63** "basking happily": Blanche Krause, "Tsk, Tsk," *Sunday Bulletin* (Philadelphia), April 1, 1956; **p. 63** "not have to depend": Kittie Campbell, "Museum Receives Grace's Gown at Champagne Gala Tonight," *Evening Bulletin* (Philadelphia), June 4, 1956; **p. 63** "an interesting idea": Letter from Henri Marceau to Mrs. John B. Kelly, February 23, 1956; **p. 63** Philadelphia Arts Week: William J. Lohan, "Thousands Flock to Museum for Start of Art Festival," *Evening Bulletin* (Philadelphia), February 26, 1955; **p. 63** "It is like having": Kittie Campbell, "Grace Kelly's Gown to Be Museum Exhibit Here," *Evening Bulletin* (Philadelphia), March 12, 1956; **p. 63** The Museum promised: Philadelphia Museum of Art press release, March 13, 1956; **p. 63** "if ever a daughter": Minutes of the meeting of the Board of Trustees, Philadelphia Museum of Art, March 7, 1956; **p. 63** voiced his pleasure: Philadelphia Museum of Art press release, March 13, 1956; also see Kittie Campbell, "Grace Kelly's Gown," *Evening Bulletin* (Philadelphia), March 12, 1956; **p. 63** "We at the Museum": Blanche Krause, "Helen Rose, Designer of Grace's Gown, Keeps The Wedding Dress Top Secret," *Evening Bulletin* (Philadelphia), April 11, 1956; **p. 63** sent to Philadelphia: Letter from John B. Kelly to Henri Marceau, April 26, 1956; **p. 63** Gimbel Brothers had purchased: Jennings, "Grace 'Look' in Windows," *Philadelphia Inquirer*, January 27, 1956; **p. 63** "lifelike": Undated Philadelphia Museum of Art press release (probably from early July 1956); **p. 64** very close to the actress's measurements: Despite Grace Kelly's reluctance to disclose her vital statistics, on March 9, 1956, the *Boston Daily Globe* published "the measurements that intrigued both a producer and a Prince" in an article by Elizabeth Bernkopf called "Grace's Trousseau Top Secret—Not So for Wedding Usher." In a discussion of her costumes for *The Swan*, the actress's measurements were given as: bust 33 1/2 inches, waist 23 inches, hips 33 inches. Also listed were the sizes for her shoes (7A, 6 1/2 in a sandal), hats (22), and gloves (6 1/2); **p. 64** "I guess brides. . . . let out": United Press, "Grace Kelly's Gown in Phila. Museum," *Punxsutawney* (Pa.) *Spirit*, June 7, 1956; **p. 64** "one of the most. . . . her greatest

role": Kittie Campbell, "Grace's Gown Given to Museum at Fashion Group Gala Event," *Evening Bulletin* (Philadelphia), June 5, 1956; **p. 64** "favorite child": Ibid.; **p. 64** "public property": "A Dressy Party," *Philadelphia Daily News*, June 5, 1956; **p. 64** "glamorous bit": Emily Belser (INS), "Grace Hasn't Changed, Dress Designer Claims," *Lima* (Ohio) *News*, July 11, 1956; **p. 64** 15,125 visitors: Libby McCall, "15,125 View Wedding Gown of Princess Grace in 1st 12 Days at Museum of Art," *Cherry Hill* (N.J.) *Herald*, July 5, 1956; **p. 66** "as soon as it": Ibid.; **p. 66** "Ladies appeared on": Ibid.; **p. 66** Visitors came: "Crowds See Kelly Gown," *Philadelphia Inquirer*, June 9, 1956; **p. 66** total visitor numbers: "Princess Grace's Cathedral Gown in Costume Wing of Art Museum," *Evening Bulletin* (Philadelphia), July 6, 1956; **p. 66** "spent several". . . . idea of the skirt: United Press, "Grace Says Art Museum Slipped Up," *Washington Post*, October 30, 1956; **p. 66** "continuing impact": "Royal Monacan Theme Adorns Fashion Group's Regal Gala," *Philadelphia Jewish Times*, March 15, 1963; **p. 66** "enhanced now": Katherine Dunlap, "Crystal Ball April 22," *Philadelphia Inquirer*, March 3, 1963; **p. 66** donated to the Museum: In 1963, Mrs. John B. Kelly donated the dress and hat worn by her daughter Margaret Davis as matron of honor and two other hats as well as the flower girl's dress worn by her granddaughter Margaret Davis. In 1997, Maree Frisby Pamp Rambo donated her bridesmaid dress to the Museum; **p. 66** major attraction: Blanche Krause, "When Brides Wore Purple Gowns," *Evening Bulletin* (Philadelphia), May 22, 1966; **p. 66** "crowning glory": Phyllis Feldkamp, "Grace's Wedding Gown Still Draws Crowds," *Sunday Bulletin* (Philadelphia), May 23, 1971; **p. 66** "a great hue": Memo from Tara Robinson to Adolf Cavallo, January 8, 1980; **p. 68** deterioration began: Letter from Mrs. James P. (Elsie) McGarvey to Mrs. John B. Kelly, May 8, 1963; **p. 68** another veil: Letter from Mrs. James P. (Elsie) McGarvey to Mrs. Helen Rose, March 19, 1976; **p. 70** "the perfect symbol": "Grace Kelly Definition of Glamour," *Mansfield* (Ohio) *News Journal*, May 27, 1956; **p. 70** "like an inverted": James S. Geggis (UP), "Large Hats Are a Sign of the Times," *Berkshire Eagle* (Pittsfield, Mass.), September 14, 1956; **p. 70** "monster-sized" handbag: Hazel Meyrick, "The Lady-like Look," *Sunday Gleaner* (Kingston, Jamaica), November 4, 1956; **p. 70** Hermès bag: Before her marriage Grace Kelly certainly owned a Hermès "haut à courroies" bag, the style that would later be called the Kelly bag; she was photographed carrying one on the day her engagement was announced. During her fall 1956 visit to the United States, the pregnant princess carried a number of different handbags both large and small; the oft-repeated story is that the Kelly bag's popularity and new name came after Princess Grace was pictured on the cover of *Life* in 1956 shielding her stomach with the bag, but no such cover seems to exist. Thanks to Francesca Picasso at Hermès of Paris for her assistance.